Seven Secrets of Modern Dating

Seven Secrets of Modern Dating

The He Said, She Said Guide for Getting from Single to Spouse

Authored & Curated by
Kirk M Samuels

Seven Secrets to Modern Dating: The He Said, She Said
    Guide for Getting from Single to Spouse

Copyright © 2022 by Kirk M Samuels

ISBN 978-0-578-34994-7
FAMILY & RELATIONSHIPS / Dating

Kirk M Samuels
Cover Design: Susan Veach | susanveach.com
Internal Design: Jeff Scott Ruiz | jsr1113@comcast.net

Dedication

My mom comes to mind as I dedicate this book to every woman trying her best to be everything she can be for her kids. Please keep going and keep pushing, as you are the unsung heroes for the next generation. I think about my father as I dedicate this book to every wounded man trying his best to live up the title in which you feel unqualified for. I see your scars and I hear your heart. The best you can do is the best you can do.

To you, the reader, you are my tribe; and I am committed to helping you push your best to be better and to have everything your heart desires.

Table of Contents

Foreword

I met Kirk Samuels at a business building conference shortly before his first book came out. I was struck by his compassion and empathy for everyone whose path he crossed. After I read his book, I understood why.

Kirk is a product of relationship trauma. Because of his character, he has used his decades on the planet to understand what happened in all of his important relationships, how to work beyond the scars, and—to the benefit of anyone reading this book—how to help others work through their own.

Importantly, Kirk is able to help beyond the *what happened?* level. He has synthesized his learning into a powerful ability to help those just starting out (or starting over) avoid the trauma to begin with. Helping others understand where their scars came from, and then preventing those issues from recurring, has become his life's mission. That is the point of this book.

Kirk and his colleagues, Paula, Genie and Jason, have created this resource for those who want to experience fulfilling life partnerships that bring joy rather than pain. Yes, those relationships exist; and these authors will help you create the mental framework to build nothing but the best in your next, and hopefully last, romantic relationship.

Mark Hardcastle
March 2022

Acknowledgments

Thank you, God, for meeting me in that dark valley and shining light so I could find my way out. Ma, the older I get, the more I understand everything it took for you to provide for us. There was so much you didn't get to do because you had two boys to take of. My life is a monument of remembrance to your sacrifice. I always wanted to make you proud and still wake up every day with that desire in my heart. I hope you see return on everything you invested in and sacrificed all those years. God knew what I needed in a mom to be what He needed me to be, and you are that mom. Thank you and I love you. You're the real best-seller. Thank you, dad, for doing the best you could. If I would've been through everything you went through, I would probably be more like you than I know.

To my kids, I know it's not easy to have a dad share some of the public things I do. I hope you can see that I'm trying to make the world a better place so no one else must go through what you did. Thank you four for your patience as I continue to grow into the man I'm trying to become.

To my big ole family, you all helped mold me into the man I needed to be to stand out in a crowded world. I love my big, loud, sometimes crazy family with all the brothers, sisters, aunts, uncles and cousins who are my safe place. People can't believe that I'm one of the quiet ones in comparison to my family.

Thank you, Norfolk State University. Behold the Green and Gold! Thank you, Art Monk, for picking a crying kid off the ground at your football camp. I hope to meet you one day to remind you of what you did for me that day. My Suitland High crew will always be in my cheering section, and I thank you for leaving no doubt of that in my soul. Thanks to PD, PT, and PL for your love and mentorship.

To my BeMen, Step Seven guys and other men who help keep me honest in my walk as a man, I honor you. Thanks, Jeff, for the dope editing and book design. You came in after a huge pivot in this book journey and did what no editor could in such a short time. Lastly, thank you to all the closed doors and rejections in relationships and dating. You helped me appreciate and recognize the gift that is the open door of light I've been able to experience. That open door of light has been a gift from God. I choose you. You are my muse.

Meet Your Authors

Kirk M Samuels
Paula Burt
Jason Kendrick
Genie Goodwin

KIRK M SAMUELS

Kirk M Samuels is known as "The Intimacy Incubator". He is a father, author, coach, gifted speaker and award-winning member of Toastmasters International.

Kirk created a class called Free Indeed, which helps those who struggle with internet pornography. He has spent years helping people get free from addiction and healing their broken relationships. His book, *For Your Eyes Only: The Inside Scoop About Men, Porn and Marriage*, reveals to women how their men can become addicted to them.

Kirk is a featured radio personality on *The Real Traci Rock Show* and *The Corner Café Radio*. He is also a board member of Step Seven Ministries, and is on the advisory council of the BeMen Foundation.

Kirk's personal mission statement: "With strength, wisdom, gentleness and mercy, I co-create a world of intimacy and unconditional connection by teaching and inspiring 1 million men how to live free from internet pornography."

www.kirkmsamuels.com

PAULA BURT

Paula is an international transformational agent, author of *Embodying the Kings Code*, co-creator of Sailing Activations, and coach who empowers individuals to expand their lives and businesses.

She has an 18-year financial planning background and a Bachelor's degree in psychology. She is a Reiki master, Access Consciousness facilitator, yoga instructor and shaman. She gleans from it all and commands the energy of spaces and bodies to vibrate at a higher level, and empowers others to do the same.

She is known to see into a soul's core and has a field of energy which allows a soul to be fully seen and accepted, to express themselves in fullness, and teaches them to create from that aligned and transparent place. The magical space.

www.paulaburt.com
www.facebook.com/paula.b.gardner/
Instagram: iam_paulaburt

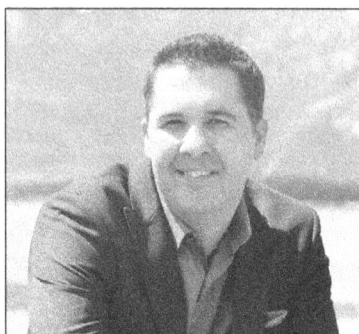

JASON KENDRICK

Jason is the author of *It's Not Your Life, It's You* (books 1 & 2). He is a transformational speaker, Reiki master, personal development coach and a co-host of the *Mad Men of Masculinity* podcast on YouTube. He lives in the Denver, Colorado area and works with the BeMen Foundation and *A Course in Miracles* communities.

As an empath, intuitive and son of a psychiatric nurse, Jason has always focused on what makes people tick and learning the why behind a person's behavior. As a certified life coach, he uses his experience and personal development training to help get to the roots of people's actions and behaviors. He helps them learn what's unconsciously driving them so they can consciously make better choices in all areas of their lives.

Jason is available as a keynote speaker, for individual and group coaching, and for workshops for organizations, businesses and groups.

www.JasonBKendrick.com
info@jasonbkendrick.com

GENIE GOODWIN

Genie Goodwin is known as "My Relationship Genie" for helping people overcome their challenges. As a relationship expert, a certified high-performance coach and best-selling author of *How to Win Her & Influence Him*, Genie believes every problem in life is a relationship problem. Her favorite thing is to empower people to overcome their challenges.

If you're a man who would like to build a healthy, passionate and long-lasting relationship with a woman, check out the *Win Your Wife Back Adventure* at **www. myrelationshipgenie.com/pl/256640**. This 30-day program trains you to get a win with her every day!

If you're a woman who wants to experience a healthy, deeply trusting, intimate and long-lasting relationship, check out *Relationship Revolution for Women* at **www. myrelationshipgenie.com/pl/36158**. Men play the game of love by completely different rules than women. Learn what they are so you won't have difficulty in your relationship.

If you'd like to talk to Genie, apply for a complimentary strategy session at **www.myrelationship genie.com/pl/2147572373**.

Introduction

Relationships and their origins have been part of the human experience from the beginning. Surely Mr. & Mrs. Cave had some exciting story about how they met. They almost certainly had different versions of how the story happened. Who made the first move? Who was more nervous? Who chased whom, and for how long? It's either each one's version or the way it really happened. As with most stories, the truth lies somewhere in the middle.

This book is unapologetically written for people who want to transition from sitting alone on their couch every evening to finding their long-term relationship. While this may not be everyone's dating goal, there is something for any single person to take away from these pages. Being single is not a disease. It's perfectly okay to be single forever or for a phase in your life.

This book is for everyone (unless you never want to date or be in a long-term relationship). We combine our personal experiences and professional insights to share wisdom and guide you to wherever you choose to take your relationship. Often, we see marriages as beginning with a ring on the finger. The truth is that engagement begins before the first day of a relationship, not when you are ready to get married.

For some of you, your engagement started when you decided to invest in this book. You could be on the path right now to having your last dating profile, your last first date or your last first kiss. This could be the beginning of your last "how we met" story. If so, be sure to include this book in the version of your story and invite us to your wedding!

MY WHY

I hate divorce. During a recent visit to my childhood home, I was compelled to reflect upon my upbringing and family dynamic through that time. Although my parents' relationship ended with legal separation as opposed to divorce, I experienced growing up in a mostly split home. In my adult life, I have seen the first hand effects of divorce on two people legally ending their marriage.

People rarely find themselves better off on paper after divorce. Some could argue commonly that getting out of a toxic relationship is benefit enough for going through the process. If someone tells you they won after the divorce, they are lying. There is always something you lose after dissolution. I have also seen first hand the effects of divorce on kids, extended family, friends, social circles and within faith communities. There's no easy way to comfortably inform any of those people, especially the kids, that a marriage is ending.

Statistically, most marriages end in divorce. A dark reality lies beneath the surface. Most divorces are a person's second, third or more. In other words, most are repeat offenders like me. Too often, divorced people will continue to do the same things and expect different results. That's insane! I would bet that most people, as they walk out of court with divorce papers in hand, could think back to how the relationship was doomed from the beginning. Younger generations see the madness and are walking away from the idea of long-term relationships and marriage altogether.

What would happen if we stopped the cycle? What are the possibilities if we took time to rethink the way we meet people, date and enter into long-term relationships? What if we started from the beginning and look at the process from there? Look, humans are wired for connection. Our default setting is for intimacy and relationship. We will not stop looking for someone to walk through life with as a romantic and intimate partner. In some cases, people have decided marriage no longer works for them, yet still seek that ideal (and possibly last) long-term partner.

Yeah, I know you or someone you know may have given up on dating because "it's too damn hard." What if it was hard because we're doing it wrong from the beginning? Could we mastermind a way to do it better? I hope to. I want to be a part of the solution and have invited a team of superheros into the mastermind. These friends not only have personal life experiences, but also work with other professionals in the space. Whether it's self-healing, personal growth, marriage, relationship building, legal or counseling, we endeavor to help write the book on a new way forward in dating within in this internet driven, post-pandemic age.

We offer ourselves as resources beyond these pages and hope to connect with each and every one of you. We will write from our own perspectives and may or may not necessarily agree with each other. None of us is perfect, but we offer our mistakes for your benefit. No one is speaking for anyone else.

As author and curator of this project, I hope you are able to find yourself on the journey laid before you and discover a new path to your next foray "from single to spouse." I trust you, dear reader, to take in the various opinions and decide what resonates with you as a new way to view the dating and relationship process. Keep the meat and spit out the bones in terms of what works for you.

HE SAID, SHE SAID

We have been good friends and colleagues for some time. We have devoted much of our personal and professional lives to helping people get out of their own way in order to have what they truly want: a healthy and successful long-term relationship. You will soon learn more about us and why we're writing this book together. We have a passion for helping as many people as possible reach their relationship goals.

Some parts of this book will feature our agreed-upon opinion and perspective. Other parts will be solely one of our perspectives. At the foundation of this book is a respect for each other's points of view and anyone with a different perspective. Some of our insight stems from what we and those with whom we've worked have done effectively, whereas other advice is gleaned from what we wish we could have done better.

At the beginning of each chapter (Secret), I will answer questions that relate to that chapter. My answers are intended to be as direct as possible. I invite you to not only agree/disagree, but also to take time to answer the questions for yourself and invite those in your social circle to share their perspectives, as well.

PIXELATED DATING

The glaring reality is that the way we approach dating has drastically changed in recent years. The evolution of desktop and handheld computers that can access the internet has changed how we interact with the rest of the world. Statistics suggest that over 44 million people have online dating profiles in the US alone.

It is quite normal to meet a two-dimensional avatar before meeting the three-dimensional person and entering into a four-dimensional relationship. With a global pandemic driving us indoors and away from groups of people for months or years, meeting someone in person could be a life or death decision! At the end of the day, though, we are still relational beings.

We have taken on the task of defining new rules for overcoming the obstacles to entering and exiting the dating process successfully. This book will be a fun and interactive guide for your journey. We will provide additional resources outside of this book to help you. We also hope to hear from you and interact with you through the journey. We have no intention of providing legal or financial advice or even counseling. Consider this material as anecdotal suggestions from people who have been there and done that.

We will use the pronouns *he, she, him, her,* as we refer to the masculine and feminine dynamic that generally exists in relationships, regardless of gender or sexual preference. It would be nearly impossible to consider every relationship experience, identity and pronoun as we write. Apply the pronouns we use to whatever dynamic exists in your case.

MEET KIRK

Before I let you in on my thoughts concerning the state of modern dating and give my input on the direction it should go, I think it's only right to share a little of my story and background. If you've read my first book, you already know the deeper parts of my story. If not, it's important for you to know some of the mountains and valleys I've journeyed and which have helped inform my life's experience.

I was born in Washington, DC, in the early 1970s. I grew up in that area for 18 years. This is significant because during this period that area became the murder capital of the world due to the crack cocaine epidemic and resulting gun violence.

My father was a Vietnam veteran. At the age of 17, he was given the option of enlisting in the US Marine Corps or going to jail after getting arrested. He spent his 18th birthday in Vietnam and came home after being permanently disabled during combat. He did not look disabled or injured, but he lost sensation in his hands and arms. Before meeting my mom, he had at least two other kids with different women. I met both siblings for the first time within the last couple of years.

After settling back home in the DC area, he met my mom. I came along shortly after. My mom worked for the phone company where she would eventually retire after 30+ years of employment. In addition to his injuries, my father had also came home with a raging drug and alcohol addiction. It would be decades later when I discovered he was convicted of rape at some point and was sentenced to St. Elizabeth's Mental Hospital. It was normal for me growing up to visit him on the weekends. When he was home, there were periods of peace interrupted by chaos and abuse of nearly every kind.

I was never really a good student in school in terms of doing the actual work. For me, going to school allowed me to escape into a world vastly different from my home. My mom enrolled me in a school in the relatively wealthy neighborhood of University Park, Maryland. Most of my friends lived in houses I could only dream of; and for them, having a mom and dad at home every night was normal. In our apartment complex, no one had a father in the house. We all learned social and relational norms from each other.

One afternoon, some of my neighborhood friends brought over a VHS videotape to watch together after school. What was on that tape altered the course of my life from that day forward. I was nine years old and introduced to pornography for the first time. I still remember the name of the movie, and I can recall images of scenes that captivated every boy in the room that day. I had no idea what it was, but I knew I wanted that feeling in my brain as much as I could get it. That became my first lover, and my virginity was lost that afternoon.

I spent the next 30 years of my life seeking the same high I got that fateful afternoon. My life and thoughts were secretly consumed with her. She was my mistress. I call her the IP Mistress, and she set the template for my sexuality. She was instantly the filter through which I would see almost any female I met going forward. She got me through the good and bad days of my life.

I found her in magazines on the bottom shelf of convenience store counters. I found her in the lingerie section of the Montgomery Ward catalog. I found her in and through girls I would find interest in. My appetite for her was insatiable and she never disappointed. When I could not find her in the world around me, I found her in my world within. I could think about her, fantasize about her, even dream about her. I did not need to invest heavily in a real or deep relationship because she required extraordinarily little from me, yet gave me so much.

I graduated high school and went to college, where I found a seemingly endless supply of females to satisfy my appetite. It became normal for me to never be fully committed to any girlfriend because the IP Mistress taught me that variety was the spice of life. If I never got attached, I never had to deal with the heartbreak when it was time to move on to the next. By the end of college, I was well seasoned in holding back my ability to survive emotionally in constant relational transitions.

When I began my career as a military officer, my last college girlfriend told me she was pregnant. Surely getting married would be the end of my relationship game of Duck-Duck-Goose, right? The IP Mistress was selfish and refused to share me with my wife. I chose my first lover over my wife and young daughter. It turns out I also chose her over my career because my relationship with the IP Mistress cost me my career. Within a couple of years, my marriage would be a casualty.

After a couple of years of being single, I met a woman that I was sure could fill the dark space in my soul. Our eventual marriage grew to include my third daughter, as well as adopting a son. Like my father's war wounds, on the surface everything looked fine. Beneath the surface, however, there was a profound disconnect in sensation and human connection.

In our 5-bedroom suburban house, the IP Mistress had her own room! It was the room I used as an office where I would spend copious amounts of hours bathing in the comfort she brought to my mind, body and soul. We were pillars of our church and extended family. Still, no one knew it was all a façade—like a backlot at Tyler Perry Studios.

As the years went by, I became more resentful and emotionally distant. I was never able to connect on a deep emotional level with anyone, not even my wife. Up until that point, I never had a completely committed and faithful relationship with any woman. This would be no different. I hated myself because I knew where this was going. I wanted to get rid of the IP Mistress after 30 years by that point, but I could never manage to shake off her control.

I was ready to quit—not only my marriage, but life completely. At rock bottom, I began to sleep in the back of my truck at night and came face to face with suicide one night.

That night turned out to be the greatest tipping point of them all. I made it through that trial and some major heavy lifting in every aspect of my life. Though that marriage did not survive, I turned everything around in my addiction to pornography. Eventually, I started teaching men and women how to get free from that addiction, following the method I developed in getting myself free. This led me to publish my first book and launch my work with teaching, coaching, speaking and writing about addiction and various aspects of relationships and the masculine-feminine relational dynamic.

By far, I have seen how we, as a culture, have devalued deep connection and intimacy. I took up the moniker, "The Intimacy Incubator," and found my life's purpose to co-create a world of intimacy and unconditional connection. I realize I went deep quickly. I did that intentionally from a man's point of view in order to:

1. Offer vulnerability to the male reader if you can identify with "yeah…me, too."
2. Help women set expectations for the kind of men they will meet along their dating journey. We all have a past. You will likely not meet a single man or woman over 30 years old with zero past struggles or life failures. Our past does not dictate our future. A broken stick can still draw a straight line.

Secret #1
Go In Before You Go Out

Kirk's Q&A

1. How do you know you're ready to get started on your partner search?

Well, I'm sure the answer is NOT when you feel ready. You'll never really feel prepared because you're a work in progress. You are ready when you make up your mind that you are willing to put in both the individual and shared effort with someone to build a deep relationship.

2. What are some basic actions to get the ball rolling?

Start with the simple things in your life that could attract or repel your ideal partner. This could be as simple as cleaning your home and vehicle so that your space makes you feel better about yourself. That feeling translates to the way you carry yourself around others. Start fixing your credit score, health, financial stability or anything else you've been putting off. Take a personal development course or entrepreneurial business training to learn new skills. Stop watching porn while you're in the dating process. Allow yourself to focus on reality as opposed to fantasy. Men: can you reflect on what your role in your past relationships has been? Women: have you healed any unresolved hurts from your past?

3. What does your end-game relationship look like?

I decided my end-game relationship is to marry for the final time in my life. I believe in marriage, even though I've messed it up multiple times in the past. I know many people who never intend to get married again but do want a life partner with whom to build a life. Knowing the goal for your end-game relationship will help guide you to the right partner.

4. What's one big sign someone is ready to commit to this process?

Not to be obvious, but buying and following the guidelines in this book seems like a great indicator! They are ready when they do the work to invest in themselves. When you truly invest in yourself, you will eventually value yourself better. Subsequently, you won't settle for less from someone else. Don't give yourself some inflated value because you think you're special or just because you've been with people (whom you don't really value) who put you on a pedestal. You are also ready when you're mentally at ease with yourself.

WHERE DO I START?

The beginning of any dating or relationship journey begins with YOU. You are the common factor in every failed relationship you have ever had. Even if you keep getting hurt by others, you must ask yourself why you keep picking bad or incompatible people. If you cannot keep a man or woman, the reason could likely be in the mirror.

Do you self-sabotage in relationships? Do you always end up getting hurt or cheated on? Do you commonly experience being ghosted? How many times have you been divorced? These are some of the things you should reflect on. You must get to *self-love*. This is totally different from *love of self*. The latter is a selfish, self-centric view of the world existing to serve you; and everything is focused on being about you, just for the sake of you. Self-Love looks in the mirror, loving *who* you see while understanding *what* you see is a continual work in progress.

You should never enter the dating scene looking

for someone to complete or someone to complete you. *Jerry Maguire* is fiction. You should strive to be as complete as possible while looking for someone to complement you as you do the same for them. Unconditional love and intimate connection are what we want at our core. Being your best will help with your confidence so that you can bring the most authentic version of yourself for another person to either fully accept or move on.

You can be secure enough in self-love that you do not need another person's validation to have a solid self-view. If you don't love yourself, you won't appreciate yourself, and you won't expect anyone else to. If you do not love your perfectly imperfect self, you will not expect or want anyone to love those zigs and zags. To that point, if someone comes along and loves your garden despite the weeds, you will find a way to sabotage or ultimately run from that type of love until you have mastered self-love.

The process of self-discovery and self-growth may reveal that you shouldn't enter a long-term relationship. In any case, it will surely help you know whether someone is compatible with you. One typical example of this is what author David Deida writes and speaks about in-depth. This is the significance of relational and sexual polarity:

> "Regardless of gender or sexual orientation, if you want to experience deep spiritual and sexual fulfillment, you must know your natural sexual essence—masculine, feminine or balanced—and live true to it. You can't deny your true sexual essence by covering it with layers of false energy for years, and then expect to know your authentic purpose and be free in the flow of love."
>
> —David Deida,
> The Way of the Superior Man

With some investment in yourself before meeting the other person, you can bring value to your first interaction. You offer them the gift of knowing, accepting and loving the whole of you. They can be the gold to help fill in the cracks in your vase.

Some practical ways you can know yourself better and invest in yourself could involve therapy to heal issues from your past. We all have baggage. When you don't unpack your baggage, it becomes luggage. You knowingly or unknowingly take it with you everywhere you go. At some point, you get used to the dead weight and forget you are carrying it. Meanwhile, the other person is unconsciously being asked to carry some or all of it. If they want to have sex with you, they may do that for a while. Usually, they will become tired of the extra luggage and leave it at the ticket counter. They would rather make their flight on time without paying for your excess weight.

It's okay to have scars from your past, but you will eventually bleed all over the person you invite into your life if you're still nursing unhealed wounds. Here are some things to consider:

- Roughly 60% of divorces involve someone with a porn problem.

(Huffpost.com, "Does Porn Watching Lead to Divorce?")

- 1 in 5 girls and 1 in 20 boys is a victim of child sexual abuse.

(National Centers for Victims of Crime)

- According to a 2015 study, women initiate 69% of all divorces.

(DivorceMag.com, "The Breaking Point: Why Do Women Initiate Divorce More Than Men?)

Besides therapy, counseling or life coaching, here are some other ways you can get to know and invest in yourself:

Myers-Briggs: The purpose of the Myers-Briggs Type Indicator® (MBTI®) personality inventory is to make the theory of psychological types described by C.G. Jung understandable and useful in people's lives. The essence of the theory is that much seemingly random variation in the behavior is actually quite orderly and consistent, being due to basic differences in the ways individuals prefer to use their perception and judgment.

Attachment Style: Attachment styles refer to the particular way in which an individual relates to other people. The style of attachment is formed at the very beginning of life, and once established, it is a style that stays with you and plays out today in how you relate in intimate relationships and in how you parent your children.

(www.simplypsychology.org/attachment-styles.html)

Enneagram: From one point of view, the Enneagram can be seen as a set of nine distinct personality types, with each number on the Enneagram denoting one type. It is common to find a little of yourself in all nine of the types, although one of them should stand out as being closest to yourself. This is your basic personality type.

Everyone emerges from childhood with one of the nine types dominating their personality. Inborn temperament and other prenatal factors are the main determinants of our type. This is one area where most of the major Enneagram authors agree—we are born with a dominant type. Subsequently, this inborn orientation largely determines how we learn to adapt to our early childhood environment. It also seems to lead to certain unconscious orientations toward our

The He Said, She Said Guide for Getting from Single to Spouse   7

parental figures, but why this is so, we still do not know. In any case, by the time children are four or five years old, their consciousness has developed sufficiently to have a separate sense of self. Although their identity is still very fluid, at this age, children begin to establish themselves and find ways of fitting into the world on their own.

(www.enneagraminstitute.com)

Adverse Childhood Experiences Score: Adverse childhood experiences (ACEs) are potentially traumatic events that occur during childhood. The Centers for Disease Control and Prevention (CDC) and Kaiser Permanente conducted the first ACE study from 1995 to 1997 and asked more than 17,000 adults about childhood experiences, including emotional, physical, and sexual abuse; neglect; and household challenges of parental separation, substance abuse, incarceration, violence, and mental illness. Nearly two-thirds of participants noted at least one ACE, and more than 1 in 5 noted three or more. Researchers identified a link between ACE exposure and a higher likelihood of negative health and behavioral outcomes later in life, such as heart disease, diabetes, and premature death.

National Conference of State Legislatures
(www.ncsl.org/research/health/adverse-childhood-
experiences-aces.aspx)

"The ACE score reveals some of our deepest historical trauma. The results provide a realistic snapshot of someone's painful past. Still, they can also prompt compassionate conversations about how that person has overcome such devastating relational pain. Both partners can reveal how early trauma has impacted adult relationships and share ongoing victories in their healing processes."
—Alex A. Avila, MA, LPC, CST, CSAT, CPTT, ACS, NCC

Before getting into the dating pool, you should spend as much time as necessary learning, growing, and investing in yourself with the help of these tools. I have provided a checklist to track where you land with the tools and assessments above. I'm calling this the Personal Discovery Roadmap. You can use it to track your introspections and see if you are compatible with someone else through their personal discovery. If you have invested in yourself by doing your work to some level and they don't share the same interest with you, that might indicate how serious that person is about developing a long-term relationship.

You are not perfect and neither is this person. However, you two can provide the Yin to the other's Yang. Healthy differences in two people who have done self-work do not amplify dysfunction. It does, however, provide the polarity for initial attraction and a long-term relationship. You can lean on each other's strengths and gifts for the mutual benefit of the relationship. For each of the assessments in the Personal Discovery Roadmap, there is a corresponding result in that same assessment that makes someone a great match for you. You may have to do a little research to find out what that is for you.

Use the Personal Discovery Roadmap
provided on the next page, OR

Download your free PDF of the
Personal Discovery Roadmap here:
www.SevenSecretsOfDating.com

PERSONAL DISCOVERY ROADMAP

Myers-Briggs Personality Type: _____

Ideal Partner Personality Type: _____

Attachment Style: _____

Ideal Partner Attachment Style: _____

Enneagram Personality Type: _____

Ideal Partner Personality Type: _____

Adverse Childhood Experiences Score: _____

BONUS CHALLENGE EXERCISE

This may be outside the comfort zone for many people, but it could provide a huge confirmation later in this journey. Once you have done the self-reflection and investment to prepare yourself for the right person to come into your life, take some quiet time to consider your unique strengths, weaknesses, personality and past experiences. Then, consider what type of person would be an ideal fit for everything you learned about yourself through the Personal Discovery Roadmap. This person has balancing strengths, weaknesses, personality and a past.

Now that you know how that person balances you and you them, write them a love letter! Yes, guys—you, too! This will only mean something if you do it before meeting the person. In life, you often find what you are looking for. Knowing what—or in this case, who—you are looking for will allow your subconscious to help you find them. Lean into your persona and be wholly you. Express yourself in whatever ways come entirely natural for you. Be as earnest, funny, sappy, dry, whimsical, detailed, free-spirited, practical, imaginative or any other way this person will get when they meet you. You can type it or handwrite it. Make it as long as you like, but put some effort into it. *Tell them everything you love about them.*

Describe their traits that bring balance and complement who you are as a person. Illustrate what you look forward to bringing them. This is not a time to bring up past hurts or disappointments. You are not re-living nightmares because this is the time to dream of the best. You've already unpacked your baggage, so they don't need to carry your past luggage. This is a love letter to who you hope is your forever person. Avoid going into great detail regarding their physical appearance. Remember, this person is likely not exactly like you. You have learned a great deal about your mental, emotional and personal makeup.

Here's the hitch: you will only give this letter to them on your wedding day (or on "you're my person" day). Don't even tell them (or anyone you date along the way) that you have this letter. It will be a complete and special surprise. Let's be real: at this point, you probably can't offer this person your virginity on your wedding day. You can, however, offer them this special gift. Again, this will come into play later in this journey. Later, you will understand why we do not want you to seal this letter in an envelope. You should keep it in a safe place where you will be able to remember and find it, even years later.

PAULA:

If I was at *Aha! I'm ready to dive into commitment and ready to find my person!*, I would start within myself and fill up every single area of my life with things that bring me joy, happiness, connection and love. Connection internally and connection to community. Connection in all ways so when I can be in communication and in partnership with somebody, I'm creating an interdependence versus a codependence.

I think many people are looking for someone else to fulfill themselves. I know I can feel that when someone is doing that to me. If you want a sustainable quality relationship, it comes from filling up your cup and being careful to say that it's not ultra-independence, either. We need each other. We're pack animals. But the pendulum has swung to the point of where we expect other people to fill up our cups for us. Then you're always, always, always in disappointment mode.

If you want to build from ground zero a sustainable relationship, you've got to have the self-respect. That is self-love. To me, self-love is self-respect. What you don't want to happen is to be so desperate for a relationship that you're willing to take anything that comes your way. We all get to be choosy without being too choosy. Be choosy with what your clearly defined yeses and noes are. Also understand we are all human. If an airplane is going down, put on your oxygen mask first. Gotta have a full cup to give, also.

Personal Work

In terms of inner work, a couple of favorite things come to mind. Any type of breathwork, EMDR (Eye Movement Desensitization & Reprocessing) or yoga is fantastic. Get to know yourself and your triggers by learning how to take a step back and decipher: *OK, is this mine? Is this theirs?* Does that really matter when you're in communication? There are times when it doesn't matter and times when it's worth it to address with someone.

In any case, doing your inner work will help clarify if something is really you or the other person. It's finding and learning about all those inner pieces, and a lot like inner child work or re-parenting. I don't know a person in this world who hasn't experienced some type of trauma. There are certain massive traumas that could come out in their relationship, for sure.

Compatibility

I've observed that most people speak through projection or mirroring, so if there's no self-awareness, you will be projecting all your crap onto your partner. You're not going to be compatible with anybody until you create that internal unlocking and redirection of the mirror and love all those pieces. That's the thing—getting rid of the self-blame and shame is vital so you don't project that.

Honestly, it becomes fun. Instead of blame, shame and complain, it becomes *What do we love doing together? What do we love creating together? Is this a person I want to grow with? Is this a person I can communicate with? Is this a person I can dance through life with?* Those are compatibility factors, and it takes two people to turn the mirror around a little bit.

JASON:

This is something that has been part of my journey, as well. Start looking back on all previous relationships. Look at what didn't work, what did work, and see if the overall theme was dramatic or not. Was there a lot of back and forth? Were there a lot of control issues? Look at those things, then realize it's neither good, bad, right or wrong. Realize you are the common denominator in each one of those areas. That can show you the patterns you have.

As you go within to figure out those patterns, take it with you. Use kid gloves. You want to be gentle with yourself, because we tend to be our own worst critic and hardest on ourselves. Or, look at your patterns and get into some counseling, therapy or personal development; or even get into some self-help books. What is the story and underlying trauma that guided you to those people in your past relationships? Why did those relationships turn out the way they did? What was the power struggle? What was the reason behind it?

Baby boomer parents who grew up in the south may not have been comfortable with emotion. Being intimate, I developed a people-pleaser mindset. That led me to be codependent, to attract damaged or traumatized women who were narcissistic. I was looking at them as if I could help them, thinking they might love me more because I helped them. That led me down a path of not having any great intimate relationships. There was a lot of emotional unavailability. Look at your past relationships. Look at your family and how they interacted. Recall if they were open, intimate, caring, bullying or not emotionally available. These will be the keys and signs along the path you travel.

These are the areas I need to look at for myself, because we inevitably want to get to a place of being a healthy relationship. I know that from my experience and from a lot of folks I've coached. We aren't really sure what a healthy relationship is. My parents didn't have a healthy relationship. We were used to it because that's how they were. We may not realize that what we had in the past wasn't healthy. Identifying the patterns that lead us away from healthy, intimate relationships and into power struggles and codependent narcissistic relationships can help with understanding our driving forces.

Our stories and our subconscious cause us to choose certain people. That may or may not be healthy, but it feels normal because that's what we're used to. We need a relationship we can grow with and create with that forever person.

As you look at yourself and think about getting off the couch and into the world to find your person, go within before you go out. Have a compassionate, loving mindset when you look at yourself, your patterns and your family. Find out what those stories are and what the traumas are. What are the energy dynamics from your family that have led you to your past relationships? What are the patterns that have led you to those past relationships? You may have learned from them, and you may be looking in the mirror thinking *What is wrong with me?* We've all had that moment, but it's not unhealthy.

Go inside. Maybe there's something I need to look at within myself. I'm the common denominator in all my past relationships and in all these struggles, and those are the things that led me to have those experiences. Now I want to understand what that story is, what that trauma is, so I can unpack it and become aware of it. In the future, I can be more self-aware, more self-loving. I can create healthy boundaries and be more authentic to myself so I can attract someone more compatible and in alignment with me.

We have chemistry. We have compatibility. These drama-trauma cycles may be what you're dealing with from past experiences and relationships. Look at your family and be an observer to your life by saying, *I wonder why this happened this way. What's the story? What's the experience I had? How can I become aware so that as I move forward I can see those unhealthy patterns and stories?*

Compatibility

There's a great book called, *The Three Compatibilities*. It's about chemistry, emotional and intellectual compatibility. At times, we tend to focus on one thing or another, depending on what our background or story is, so the chemistry is really the emotional and energetic spark. There's fire. If you've had those experiences, they burn fast and hot, then they go out. There's a lot of chemistry. There's a lot of energy. There's a lot of fireworks. It may not last very long.

Then there's emotional compatibility. You understand each other. You get each other's emotional makeup. You understand how the other person sees things, so you can be very empathic to each other.

That may or may not lead to a long term committed relationship; it may be more of a friendship or family kind of thing, but you get each other. You may have compassion and empathy for each other, but there may not be that spark. Intellectual compatibility very much comes from what you believe in.

What are you passionate about? What are the things that get you out of bed in the morning? Does this person fall in line with that? Does this person run in the same lane? Do they have the same religious beliefs? Do they have the same political beliefs? Do they have the same passions in the world? Are they athletic or artistic, musical or business minded? Do they want to save the planet? Do they like to travel? These are some of the things that can be part of the intellectual compatibility we'd ideally like to find.

Emotional and intellectual compatibility are the two main foundational building blocks that will get you to a long term relationship because the chemistry, sparks and fireworks are only going last so long. They might get you on a date or in bed with that person, but it may not get you down the aisle, into a home or into a family with that person. As powerful as the chemistry can be, it's really the foundational blocks of the emotional and intellectual compatibilities that get you into a long term relationship.

This is the person after the fireworks are over. After that spark has burned out, there will be a long period on which to build something. You'll have someone who understands you emotionally and intellectually. You can build things together on common ground and become very aware of your own passions and desires—and be vulnerable enough to express them.

As you get out in the world and start dating, it's not a bad thing to judge whether a person is emotionally or intellectually compatible with you. You'll just save them and yourself the time. *Oh well, we don't really match this way; but she's cute, so I'm gonna…* Don't pay attention to that. *I'm going to ignore this for the time being because I think she's cute and there may be some future here.* Don't ignore those things. In the long run, you don't want to think, *I'm going to get with this person cuz she's cute and I'm just blown,* out of loneliness, low energy or depression. Start to become more self-aware and more grounded in who you are and don't edit that.

The quickest way to find someone who is really, truly compatible with you is to be unapologetically 100% yourself and still have boundaries. The person who agrees with those things will be the one you can work with because he/she is the one with whom you have the most to work with. Build with the most foundational pieces. It will be a determining factor if you've had traumatic relationships in the past.

This new person with emotional and intellectual

compatibility will be more understanding and have more empathy. It may feel too good to be true. *How can this person like the same things I like and think the same way I think and want to do many of the same things?* That's really what you're looking for. It's someone who fits with you, fits with your passions and intellect, and has that same foundational piece you can build with. In the long run, those are the things that are going to sustain you through the tough times and through the years. This will be someone you want to create a life with and a family in the future.

GENIE:

Always start your actions with your *why* because this is where your clarity and power come from. Unfortunately, humans usually start with *how* instead of *why*. This makes it easy to get off track or be beat up by the process. Sit down and think about why you want to start dating. What would be the end result you want to achieve from dating? Write a list of all the things you want to experience so that brilliant brain of yours can focus on it in the journey and make sure you experience it. This clarity will determine how you move through the dating process.

For instance, some people want to date in order to have fun; that's their whole purpose for dating. You need to know if that's what you're after because that may not be somebody else's *why*. If you truly want to end up with your lifelong partner, it will determine how you're going to move through the dating process, so just get really clear on what your own personal *why* is. This clarity will show you how to move through your dating process with less kerfuffle and pain.

I like to say relationships are the crucible of personal development. What you discover in a relationship journey, dating or married, is everything that matters to you in life. You're either going to find that it's in there or not. When it's in there, it becomes the most fulfilling part of your entire life; and when it isn't, it becomes the most painful part of your entire life. So expect that.

The journey is going to make you look at yourself, what you really want, and how you really want to show up in your life. *Now I know why I want a date. Now I know how I want to show up in the journey of dating.* Those two pieces are vastly important to figure out, and that clarity allows the best experiences to come from your relationships. Always start with your *why*, then with who you are and who you want to be in that relationship.

At the beginning of a dating journey, think through the experience you want to have, and also decide how you want to show up and treat the other person. This moves you out of being a victim and into showing up as your best self. You know you're probably not going to find your person on the very first date, or even with the first person you meet.

I like to think how I want to treat the other person when they're not my person—you know, not ghosting them, not cutting them off because they're not the right person, not juggling them as if something is wrong with them because they aren't your fit, just really being your best self in the journey and making sure that when a person isn't the right fit for you that you handle it with your highest level of integrity. You acknowledge the heart of another person who's not for you, and you handle them that way. Model a lot of integrity in the journey, and you'll transform the journey for yourself while avoiding a lot of pain and rejection.

It Can Happen Anywhere

I met my husband while standing in line at the Department of Motor Vehicles, so you can meet someone anywhere. At 17, I was young and going into my senior year of high school. I was buying my first vehicle on my own. The most handsome man I'd ever seen was standing about 15 people ahead of me. We played that "Looky Loo" game. He'd look at me and I'd look away. I looked at him and he looked away. The DMV lines are notorious for being long, so it lasted 45 minutes. He was ahead of me, so when he finished his business he walked out the door.

I was heartbroken because he was easily the most handsome man I'd ever seen in my life. Everything in my body had reacted to him. My knees started shaking and my hands started sweating. I thought, *What just happened to me?* Then he walked out the door. The devastation of it all! 15 minutes later, he came back in, walked right up to me and said he'd like to talk to me when I was through, if that was okay. I said yes, then he turned around and walked right back out the door.

It can really be a roller coaster ride on this journey, especially when the attraction goes off the charts. It goes back to showing up as your best self and handling the heart of another person really well and with great integrity. People are what this life is all about. Anyway, I finished my business about 30 minutes later and walked out the door. He was waiting outside for me and asked me out on a date. After one month of dating we were engaged; it was really fast. Basically, I married a stranger who I was madly in love with.

A lot of the things I'll talk about here happened in my marriage. I married a stranger, but I knew he was the one; so I was committed to spending the rest of my life with him and discovering the relationship process. I was going to do this for the rest of my life and so was he. Once we realized that, we were willing to commit.

Secret #2
Cast a Wide Net: Get in the Pool

Kirk's Q&A

1. I'm ready to cast a wide net. How do I start fishing?

Everyone who goes fishing begins by preparing for the task. Most importantly, do something! Nothing good is coming to you on the couch, eating Flamin' Hot Cheetos and watching reality TV! Get up, get better, get out, get social. Do something you like doing. Even if you don't find your ideal match, you'll probably meet some wonderful folks. It's easy to get caught up in life's bustling cycles, hoping the right person will just bump into you like in some romantic comedy. That's fiction, folks! You're not going to run into your Matthew McConaughey, Morris Chestnut, Kate Hudson or Meagan Good in your living room unless you're binging Netflix.

2. What are some common mistakes people make out of the gate?

Many people get too caught up in the menu and not the actual dish. Don't just order based on the pictures without checking out the ingredients. There may very well be something you're allergic to in that dish! Also, this is a marathon, not a sprint. You'd be among the rare few who find their person right out of the gate. You must be willing to toss the wrong ones back into the ocean while you continue to search for the right one to bring back to port. There are many people out there who are all frosting and no cake. They'll just leave you with a cavity and an upset stomach.

Guys, stop "simping"! Chasing after women who don't want you makes you look like a fool. Save your Likes for someone who deserves your Loves. If she doesn't respect you or if she requires you to up your game from the beginning, she's probably going to dump you at some point and leave you heartbroken.

3. What do men and women initially look for when searching for a mate?

Men look for someone to be their biggest cheerleader. Every movie you've seen with a strong male hero has included a woman as part of his story. Men get paid millions of dollars to play a sport in front of tens of thousands of fans, and they still have cheer-leaders on the sidelines. He wants her to be visually and sexually appealing but not a cheap trick! He wants to feel respected and supported. Ideally, a safe lap to lay his head on when he's taking a break from fighting his dragons.

Women want a man they can respect. Yes, she wants to be physically attracted to him; but a man with drive, passion and purpose is hot to most women. She has to be able to trust him and feel safe around him. He shouldn't *need* her, but he should want to invite her into an adventure he's already on. The modern woman can do it all, but she doesn't always want to *have* to do it all. She counts on him to carry the load and burden she would rather not carry.

4. I've cast my net, but I haven't caught anything. Now what?

Change ponds. Maybe you're looking in the wrong places. Get into multiple social circles like work, church, dating websites, sports leagues, professional networking, public speaking clubs, volunteer orga-nizations, or even a favorite park to go for walks. Don't go to these places just to hook up, but consider them opportunities to meet people in general. You may meet someone who knows just the right per-son for you. It's okay to take breaks, just don't quit. Stay open as you move about your day. You never know when the next room you walk into or event you attend might reveal the person you've been waiting for. Even introverts can enjoy going on solo hikes or activities with small groups of people. Give it some time. The biggest fish are often in the deepest waters. Be patient. Be persistent.

WHERE DO I LOOK FOR HER/HIM?

Your dating world is an ocean, and you are a fishing trawler. As you set off from the home port, you have no idea what lies beyond the harbor. A trawler is a commercial fishing boat that casts its nets as it streams across the ocean. The fishing nets are pulled behind it, and the fish are scooped into them as it moves ahead. At the end of the day, or sometimes at the end of each leg of the journey, the nets are hauled in and sorted by the fisherman as they examine the catch. After a time, the fishing boat returns to the port to unload the catch and reap the rewards.

Most commercial fishermen are looking for a specific type of fish. They are intentional in the task. Before leaving the port, the fishing crew prepares the boat and the nets for the task ahead. They fish in specific waters at specific times and with specific nets. This means that after they pull in the nets on each pass, they determine what to keep and what to throw back for someone else—or, maybe for a later catch after they grow more. Depending on what they're fishing for, they can arrange their nets to trawl along the bottom or at different depths.

Similarly, before you head out to catch your delicious delight, you should prepare yourself and your nets for your desired catch. *[See Secret #1].* Once on the mission, it's vital to intentionally cast a wide net. Catching too much in your net is not a problem you should worry about. You must be willing to sort through your net and toss back what is not for you. You should place yourself in a position to find or be found by that special someone. Rarely does that perfect relationship come to you sitting on the couch every night. Be honest with yourself if you find red flags too quickly and too frequently.

Professional daters get addicted to the novel high that comes with new people. It's like going on a shopping spree with the full intention of returning everything you bought. Don't waste other people's time pretending to be looking for a *mate* when all you want is a *date*. At least be clear up front if that's all you're looking for. There are websites for that, too.

You can do the rod and reel fishing method by paying someone to look for what you think is your perfect match. This is more costly and not necessarily a more foolproof approach for most. Commonly, matchmakers use social media or the internet in some way to vet qualified candidates, anyway. If using a matchmaker is your strategy, however, you need to be even more diligent about the self-work described in *Secret #1*. This is so you can most effectively communicate your ideal match to your matchmaker.

If he's not willing to put in some *effort* to meet you, it may indicate his level of effort to keep you. Conversely, if she has no investment up front, she might expect you to constantly cater to her needs going forward.

"If they ain't tryin', you ain't buyin'!"
— **Kirk**

The internet has generally simplified the process for meeting people. Dating websites are a great way to cast a wide net. There are tens of millions of people with profiles on any number of dating websites. Some of these sites are generic, while some are geared toward people with certain interests or backgrounds. Most sites allow you to enter as much or as little information about yourself as you wish. Photos are an expected part of any serious profile.

Profile Advice for Him

Men's dating profiles generally fall into two categories. Either you share way too much, or you share next to nothing.

Guys, it's important to understand that women do not think in the same way most men do. If you're a good guy intending to date for a good purpose, you may be tempted to go overboard with your dating profile. If you're anything like me, you may think it's better to show all your cards up front so she can see how great of a guy you are. More is not necessarily better. It's better to be effective rather than working harder to get what you're looking for. Feel free to reach out to me and allow me to help coach you through setting up a dating profile to get the results you're seeking.

PAULA:

For me, as long as you're having fun with it, then cool. If not, turn it off. Have control of this. I've been on dating apps. At times, I'd say I was done with it and just turn it off for a day or two. That comes from being involved in other things that you love to do, whether it's yoga, hiking, farming, etc. There have been times in my life when I've completely shut off wanting a relationship and then completely open to one. Know when you're shut off or when you're open—then stay open. People will naturally be drawn to that because we're all feelers; we can all tell if someone's shut off or open.

There are options for places to meet your person. Dating apps and group activities are two. There are organizations where you can sign up to go hiking or other activities, for example.

If you're building an online dating profile, create clarity and have fun. I think sometimes it's either too serious or it seems people are hiding behind fake masks. What I mean by creating clarity is to be real about it and just have fun with it. Be okay with yourself first. We're all different, but for me it's about a man who knows who he is and who knows himself. Someone who doesn't take life too seriously is important to me, too.

JASON:
The best way to meet and find people with whom you may be compatible is, first and foremost, to get off internet dating and the dating apps. Close them down. Delete them. They are a terror in the dating world, and you will spend a lot of energy for no return. Get out into the real world to meet people you'd be compatible with. Now that you've done the inner work, you know what you're passionate about.

What gets you going? Do those things and it could become your sport, your hobby. You can be you. If you like to cook, take cooking classes. There are plenty of singles groups and places you can get out to, but I find a lot of times they're just kind of throwing people together. You don't even know if they have similar backgrounds or interests. Maybe you could get out and volunteer somewhere, if that's something you're passionate about. For example, Habitat for Humanity or a community garden often have other people with similar interests; you'll be able to meet them organically.

I think we really lost a lot in the past 20-30 years with all the dating apps and online stuff. It's become a "swipe left and right" mentality. There's not much opportunity in getting to know someone or going to a place where people have common interests. Find things you are interested in and get out there and do them—not because you're trying to reach somebody, but because you enjoy it.

When you're passionate about something you're living and doing, you will become more of yourself and more attractive. The light inside you will shine and you will meet more compatible people. So find things that have less to do with more traditional singles activities than something that gets you passionate or gets your heart pumping.

Whether it's a sport, cooking or an art activity, find something you're passionate about and get yourself around similar people. Maybe you'll find someone and go out with them. Do some volunteer work or do something you enjoy. Even if you don't find something at first, someone could introduce you to a friend of theirs. That could be a path because birds of a feather flock together. If you're looking for emotional or intellectual compatibility, you'll want to be around those same people and organically find someone to be compatible with.

Get away from the false digital app dating environment and get out into the world among like-minded people with the same passions and interests. That's the best way I would say it. Be your authentic self and attract someone who's attracted to you. So get out and do the things you love to do, and meet others who do them, as well.

Digital Dating

There are over 40 million people currently using dating apps. If you still prefer to be on the platforms, I would ask how that's working for you? If it's not working for you, maybe you should consider different options. It's time to be as authentic as you can when it comes to dating apps, but you can also be positive.

Being human, I sometimes get on the apps when I'm bored. I see so much of *I don't want this* and *I don't want that* and *I'm not going to put up with this* and *I'm not gonna put up with that*. Well, great! Now, I know what you don't want, so what do you want? How do I know if I'm even your person? You know, maybe I don't fall into those categories you said "no" to. So now, how do I know what you want?

Be very proactive and positive with your profiles if you're going to be on a dating app. Do your research and get on the right dating app for you. If it costs money to join, then so be it. It's going to be money well spent, but make sure you're on the best dating app that fits your personality and your criterion of the partner you want to meet. Then, be positive and authentically yourself. If you're a Trump supporter or Biden supporter, if you're a Christian or Muslim, if you like this and don't like that, just be who you are and do it more positively.

We see so much of *I don't want this* and *I don't want that*. Great, what do you want? Let's talk about what you really want. If you're divorced and want to have a family and more kids, let's talk about that. If you're single and never married but you want to have a family and kids, put that out there. That way, you can more quickly filter through all those people who aren't a match for you.

I've seen a lot of YouTube videos on dating profile advice. They tell you all the generic things. Do this, do that. Take this picture. Put up this kind of profile. Put up this kind of heading to grab people's attention. That's marketing, not relationships. You want to be as much of yourself as possible so the right person will be attracted to that.

I think a lot of times we get lost in the minutiae and try to create click bait for ourselves. That's not actually going to get you to a real person who genuinely likes you, so be as authentic as you can. If that person is on there, they'll be attracted to you. That's the best advice I can give for digital dating. I think it needs to go the way of the dodo.

GENIE:

Online Dating

I've coached many people who are doing online dating, and one of the biggest challenges is that it's very easy to not be real—to concoct a story of who you'd like to *be*, but not *how you really are*, even by using very old pictures of yourself. No one is perfect all the time. Personally, I think the goal of perfection is a painful trap; it's just not real or possible. What you really want to know about the other person is how they handle the hard times! You want to share what your triggers are and how you are growing because of them.

The whole goal of dating is to create a real relationship, so be real or you may set yourself up for some painful times. Be willing to be real from the get-go. There's a really great process for when you're looking to hire an employee. You deliberately want to throw bombs in the way to see if they'll step up or go away. You actually want to put a little pressure in the relationship to see how they will respond, so be as real as possible. Give some pressure to see if they're going to walk away or if they're intrigued. If they step up, you really want to explore being in a relationship with them because they care enough about you to walk through your imperfections with you. That's what you're after, because we all have those, right? So be real online and on your web page and in your conversations. Be real in your texting back and forth. Aim for a real relationship and a real face-to-face as soon as possible.

Secret #3
Put Down the Mouse and Get Out of the House

Kirk's Q&A

1. How do you go from virtual to in-person meetings?

Be bold. If you're meeting someone in a dating setting like a website or singles event, don't hesitate to initiate a conversation with someone. Fellas, text relationships don't count. The more you text, the more you turn her off. Digital communication should be used primarily to arrange in-person meetings, especially in the beginning stages. I'm not saying be intentionally rude or cold in text, but she will only see you as a viable partner when you meet. Even if the female initiates offline contact, she would usually prefer not to be the primary driver of early stage in-person meetings.

A simple "Hello, my name is…" would be a great ice breaker approach. "Are you single?" is a great way to clarify interest. "Can I call or text you?" is a straightforward way to see if they are interested in the next step. Ideally, those aren't the only three things you could say and hope for success. If their interest in you is not obvious, feel free to disengage and move on politely. **If they are interested, it's on them to make it clear after you have initiated.**

2. How do I get a second date with someone I'm interested in?

First, if they are not *really* interested in a second date, you don't want one. **They should be just as interested as you, and they should make it clear.** Most people in modern dating are clear with interest. If a woman is on a first date with a man, she's already indicated the slightest curiosity to find out more about him. The first date is not for anyone, especially the man, to perform or convince the other person he/she has value.

A man of value demonstrates it through his persona while in her presence. Likewise, a woman will demonstrate something of substance to offer a man. If you are each other's cup of tea, it will be sweet tea. With all of that being said, it's totally appropriate at the end of the first date to say that you would love to get together again sometime soon. If there is an **enthusiastic** agreement, agree to reach out in the next day or two *with a plan* for the next date.

3. How do I know when to cut bait?
Cut bait when the juice isn't worth the squeeze. I believe the masculine should forever pursue the feminine. It is the responsibility of the feminine to reciprocate; however, when you find yourself continually seeing their back, you are chasing them. When you hear an echo, you know that what you sent out is returning from something facing you. You should expect to be putting in an effort. You should also expect to see action from the other person.

4. How do I know when this might be a keeper?
They are a keeper when you feel like you're not only giving of yourself but also returning what you receive from them—when they are as excited and interested as you, *and* they make as much effort as you do to grow the connection into something more. Once you feel this, time will tell if this is the longer-term person for you.

I'M INTERESTED IN THIS PERSON. NOW WHAT?

Once you have established mutual interest, it's time to take the communication offline. This involves texting, talking and virtual dating. This phase does not have a set time frame or time limit, but it is important like sorting through your net.

This phase will help you decide if there is enough shared interest in the first date between the two of you. Whoever is considered the most masculine should take the lead and ask for a phone number. Reach out when your heart tells you to. If it's right, they will be on the same timeline.

Besides initial greetings, the goal is not to get into long texting conversations. Without being rude or pushy, the goal is to plan a dedicated time for a meeting. The earliest conversations should occur over the phone or video call. (Men, remember that the more you text in the beginning, the less attractive you become to her.)

When you're both comfortable, plan an initial face-to-face meeting in public for as soon as you both are available. Whoever asked for the phone number should continue to take the lead in scheduling the first date. Have a plan for where to meet and what the activity will be.

The masculine should plan the first date somewhere familiar and where he's comfortable paying. Also, consider getting coached on conversational dating or joining a public speaking club if you aren't comfortable expressing yourself verbally. You don't have to become a public speaker, but most women connect initially through conversation and non-creepy eye contact. Working on yourself before dating and being secure in your life's purpose will give you something to say when the time is appropriate.

Men, you have two ears and one mouth, so on your first date with her you can listen more than you talk. You should have something to say when appropriate, but this is your time to learn about her. If she's on a date with you after following this plan, she is likely already somewhat interested. You have passed the first phase. The first date is to see if there should be a second date. She is just as nervous as you. Being your confident, non-cocky self will allow her to be herself.

If the first date goes well, allow it to end on a good note and agree to continue communicating and hopefully plan to get together again. Communicating offline with the primary goal of setting the next date should be repeated until either communication dies off or the connection develops to a more serious level. Both people should make an effort to keep the communication progressing; however, the masculine should mostly lead in planning at first. Great dating ideas can be found online.

Get Out of the Pool
If your true intention is a lifetime relationship, at some point you must get out of the dating pool.

Being in the pool can be addictive at times. Some might struggle with a scarcity mindset in dating, meaning they think there are only a limited number of people and options for finding a mate.

Often, we see our baggage as limitations to possibilities of who could be interested in a long-term or lifetime relationship with who we see in the mirror. A broken stick can still draw a straight line, and a broken clock shows the correct time twice a day. Don't underestimate the value of imperfections. You have all the right things to offer the right person. There is someone who zigs where you zag. Someone is the Nutella to your animal cracker.

The opposite of the scarcity mentality is an abundance mentality. This is the belief that there are enough options available to find the right person for you. Despite what you might think, abundance is more of the reality in the dating field than scarcity. The downside of scarcity is settling for the wrong person and overlooking far too many red flags.

The downside of abundance gone too far is becoming addicted to meeting new people and never getting out of the dating pool. Some people stay on dating websites for years. Not because they can't find someone, but because it's fun to meet new people and go on first dates. The "bigger-better" dater thinks the next person they meet could be better than this person. Let's face it, some people just enjoy getting free meals and coffee. Be wary of the person who likes over-the-top and fancy first dates. This is not a TV show. One-on-one dates involving private concerts, private jet flights to Vegas or hot air balloon rides to a fancy picnic on a remote mountain top are not the reality for most people.

Quite simply, the more dates you go on with a person and the more you mutually invest in communication and connection, the less you should be on the dating sites or singles mixers. At some point, dating profiles should be taken down and singles outings should fade away. If you aren't compelled to make yourself less available to other singles, it's probably a good indication this person is not the one for you.

Social Life

In these early stages, you may find that the two of you can't get enough of each other. Long phone conversations, texting throughout the day and spending copious amounts of time together is common. Don't be afraid of this desire. When there is effort and balance from both sides, these are all indications that connection is developing.

You are beginning to get to know each other. You may start to open deeper levels of vulnerability. In healthy connection building, both may gradually share past experiences, family history and future dreams. In many early relationships with great chemistry, this can happen quickly. Things can graduate to deep feelings of attachment.

This is a great time to have explored attachment theory and know where you fall in that continuum. Use discernment to not move too quickly to the deepest parts of your personal vulnerability. Allow the attachment to cook more in the intimate crockpot than the intimate microwave. Secure, long-term attachment is developed over time. This is not a sprint; it's a marathon. Allow time to reveal the person who earns your trust.

A great way to allow the relationship to simmer is to maintain some sort of extended social life and social circle outside of the relationship. Ideally, you had a full life before dating, and this included friends, family and professional circles before you met this person. Don't abandon them just because you have a new person in your life. In fact, you both should intentionally make time for those circles outside of the relationship and encourage the other person to do the same.

This is also the case after marriage, if you get to that point. The obvious exception here is when outside circles involve counter-productive activities to the relationship. You should probably not hang out with the crew that likes to hit the strip club if that causes problems with your partner.

PAULA:

I'm going to speak candidly about this. I will not ask a man out. I'm not the seeker or the hunter, but that's just me. I'm not saying it's wrong or right or bad or good. That's just my preference now. Four years ago I probably would have. Five years ago I was just getting in touch with my feminine aspect. I just won't seek any more, so I'll just wait for that invite. If an invite doesn't happen, I'll quickly move on.

I think this is where a lot of women get hung up. *Oh my gosh, what's wrong with me? What did I do wrong?* Do the internal work of releasing all that blame and shame, and love yourself completely. You won't put that pressure on men, either. It's the same aspect on different sides of the coin. Indications of a potentially good partner are:

- Communication
- Clarity
- Just having fun together

With those three building blocks you can create anything, like fun, chemistry and good communication. If a woman is interested, you likely notice:

- She says yes!
- Eye contact
- If there's chemistry and things are flowing.

If a woman is interested, she has a responsibility to make it known. No one is a mind reader. It's not fair to put that ball in someone's court and expect them to be. This is where getting clear about your yeses and noes is important, too. It's important because if you honor your noes you can honor someone else's noes. It's not hard. You can voice your opinion, desires, wants, needs, or whatever. If something is a no, that just allows a deeper depth of communication without argument.

If you're out on a first date, have genuine curiosity about the other person. It doesn't matter who I'm sitting across from. I am genuinely curious about this person, whether they're a friend, a potential partner, a business partner, or anyone else. It's a genuine curiosity. The possibility of questions is endless. I can't swim in the shallow side; it's just not who I'd be. Ask them to describe themselves and talk about their passions.

We get caught up in too much *What do you do?* I ask them to tell me what brings them joy and what their upbringing was like; where they're from and what they liked or didn't like about that area; who their friends and colleagues are, and whether or not they like to create things. After the first date, forget anything you've ever heard about how long to wait to call. Do what feels right to you. Otherwise, you're playing games. For example, *Don't call back for two days* or *Don't text back for 24 hours* is playing a game.

Trust yourself. If you make mistakes, then cool; learn from them and try again. We're all going to make mistakes, but there are no rules or regulations to communication. The best type is authentic communication, not something like *I'm gonna wait two days because this book says to*. When you feel you have to follow a rule, it can create anxiety.

JASON:

If you're really committed to finding the one best compatible for you, become very aware. Look in the mirror ask yourself, *Am I attracted to this person because they meet past criteria? Am I trying to meet this person because they're like the ones before?* A lot of times we're much more attracted to those who meet a pattern that we've been running with for many years. Become very aware of that, because the last thing you want to do is step back into that little pool or that old river and go down for that ride again. Done it before.

If you find someone you're interested in and they're not part of that past pattern, get into a very authentic conversation about who you are, who they are, what your boundaries are, and what your likes and dislikes are. If they're the right person for you, they'll be on board.

Many times, we hear that you should shoot for compromise, but there are a lot of times I think we misunderstand compromise. We give up our core beliefs or core desires because we think we need to compromise these things. If you compromise the important foundational things, you're not going to have the relationship you want. You're going to continue to compromise, and that will most likely end in a dramatic and traumatic finish.

As you meet people you're attracted to and interested in, find out what level of compatibility you're on. Is it the chemistry, or are they just hot and you have nothing new to talk about the next day? Is this someone you have emotional compatibility with—who understands your emotional makeup and with whom you also have intellectual compatibility? You can have these conversations, and there's also that feeling of intimacy and closeness with them, because at the end of the day we define what intimacy and love really are. What we all want is to find someone we can be 100% unedited with all the time, good, bad or ugly. They would love us because of that, not despite that.

If you're out on a date with an attractive person and they are displaying red flags, you may feel you have to compromise. Don't waste any time. Save yourself and move on to someone else. At the end of the day, we're all looking for intimacy—being 100% yourself with someone else. Do that as much as you can and as soon as you can when someone is interested. You don't want to waste six months or a couple of years with someone, only to find out that person isn't the right one for you because you've been edit-ing yourself. You'll discover core dynamics and core belief systems that just don't resonate.

If you're interested in someone, be as much of yourself as you can. See how they respond to that, and if they don't respond well, there's no diminish-ment on you or on them. It's just not your person. Move on and try to find someone with whom you can be yourself.

A good potential partner would be someone who shares your interests and who has some of the same core values. We hear this thing about opposites attracting; and if you look at it materially, you real-ize that when we say opposites attract, it's the mas-culine-feminine energies that attract. It's those core beliefs, core passions and drives that need to be in some kind of alignment, or harmonious energy.

Another sign of a potential partner is someone who accepts you as you are. The more you open up the more they like you. The more you're around, the more comfortable you feel about being yourself. It's back to being 100% yourself. Intimacy with some-one means you love them exactly for who they are, warts and all; and they love you exactly for who you are, warts and all. You have those core foundational things that you can build on.

As you're out in the world, if you find yourself editing or biting your tongue or walking on eggshells, that's not your person. You want to be yourself as much as possible with the right person. They will feel the same way. The most loving thing you can do is to be accepting and understanding of someone. If you're with them and it feels like work, if their boundaries feel like work to you, it's not your person. You want to find that person who seems to fit with you so you can be yourself, relax and just be with them, no matter what.

There are signs when men and women are interested. There's chemistry and flirtations. If they see something in you they want, they may be giving you attention or they want to be around you. What I'm starting to realize from my own experience is that when someone seems to be compatible, we may notice only an interest because it's not the fireworks we're looking for. We all want to have those fireworks; however, fireworks tend to burn out very quickly, and that's not what tends to build healthy relationships.

There's so much foundational common ground. Find someone who's interesting to you and who has the same common ground. Do they want to be around you? Will they put in the effort? Will they check in on you? See if they want to get to know you, and not just for how much you make, how tall you are or where you can take them for Christmas. See if they're interested in your past experiences or your family history or your pet—the things that made you who you are.

I'll say this for the ladies, but this can also pertain to men as well: Sometimes you want to look in your friend zone for those people who are generally interested in who you are. They are the ones who will make better potential matches in the long run. Do you want the long run? Do you want a family? Those are the people who share a lot of your core values, and one may end up being that special person.

First Date Questions

One of my favorite people questions to help weed through the chaff very quickly is: "What are your past traumas and what are you doing to heal those so that you don't put them on me?" During the first few days, I would cut through the BS very quickly.

Maybe it's the second date. You want to get to the core of who they are very quickly because this is not a long-term dating strategy. You're looking for a long-term partner strategy. The quicker you can go through those who don't make the cut and those who don't match with you, the better off you will be, especially on first dates. Be authentically yourself and ask questions that pertain to your interests. Are they interested in the same things you are? Do they have the same political ideology or religious ideology? Do you agree on many of the same things?

If you differ in many categories, no matter how cute they are, this may not be the person for you; so don't take things personally. You're looking to quickly weed through those who don't match with you so you can get a better match and create that beginning with them.

Waiting to Call or Text

This one makes me crazy because I think it's very much dependent on you and that person. There are all these theories about two to three days. I think it's all just a game and about trying to be emotionally unavailable because they don't want to be hurt. If this is someone you're attracted to and interested in, and if you both have the same common core connections and beliefs, follow your gut.

If you text or call them the next day and want to have a connection with them, but they're not on the same page or they judge you for contacting them too soon or too late, that may not be your person. I don't think there should be any hard and fast rule about how long to wait. I think a lot of that is just dating politics. If there's someone you really connect with and feel you can be yourself with, they're going to want you to connect with them whenever you feel like it. Follow your heart when it comes to how much you connect.

GENIE:

Intimacy is the best thing that makes a great relationship. Intimacy is what you're after, and I'm not necessarily talking about sex. I'm talking about emotional intimacy, where you can really be yourself. You can be authentic and you can be real, so share the real you in the beginning. You absolutely want to show up as your best self, but we're not always our best. None of us live our lives at the highest and best version of ourselves at all times; that's why it's vital to share all the parts of you. Find out how someone handles stress, how they handle being cheated on, how they leave a relationship, what they think of their family and what the deal breakers are.

On the first date, I would absolutely talk about why I was dating and what I was after in order to find out if they're on the same page. If she's looking for marriage and he's looking for fun, he's not going to have any. Just get real explicit on that very first date. Talk about what your deal breakers are and what you really want in a relationship.

I have coached clients who don't want to have sex until they're married. I've also coached clients who want to have sex just for fun. Knowing what your wants are and what's acceptable to you is really important before you even begin a relationship.

The other thing I'd say is that women and men

date differently. Women actually don't date men. The minute you ask a woman out on a date, she's in a relationship with you right then and there. In her mind, she's already in a relationship with you. She's judging the relationship by how you are building it and relating to her. For men, a date is typically a fun time. It's an opportunity to get together and maybe even get to know each other. He may or may not even be in a relationship yet. It's vital you are explicit with each other to avoid a world of pain that could happen when we assume what's going on.

In fact, I had one client who had been seeing a woman for two years. She began talking to him about marriage. He was frustrated and said to me, "We aren't even dating yet!" They had been physically intimate with each other the entire time, but in his mind he wasn't even dating yet. I found out that previously this man had been through a horrible divorce. He made the decision that he never wanted to marry again, but he didn't share that decision with her. So in his mind, they weren't even dating yet. These things are really important in beginning to understand each other, preferably in the very beginning. Otherwise, you end up assuming things about each other that may be nowhere near accurate.

Intimacy requires understanding and authenticity, so be understanding and authentic rather than judgmental. Hopefully, you're going to see that coming back at you. Most people can pick up on it if it's real, but it makes the whole process much easier and less painful if you simply and explicitly talk it out.

Secret #4
Be Exclusive

Kirk Q&A

1. What do I consider exclusive?

I consider exclusive to mean we are no longer dating or romantically communicating with other people—when we have moved out of all the dating spaces we were once in. This means no more dating sites, matchmaking, bar/club scene without each other. We should keep our platonic friend circles that do not conflict with this intimate relationship, and your partner should feel secure even when you're with those groups.

If either cannot close the door to past single scenes and people, they are likely not ready to be exclusive. Don't waste time pretending to be exclusive if you're not fully ready to let the single life go.

2. **What are some signs that you two are not exclusive?**

They cannot break away from the novelty of dating sites. They still need to hang out at old (or new) hookup scenes. They still need to date other people. They are secretive with phone usage or whereabouts. They cannot say with certainty that they are exclusive. It's either a *Hell yeah!* or it's a *No*. You don't want someone who's only partly exclusive, such as refusing to introduce you to the people closest to them, like family and friends.

3. **How do you know you have become exclusive?**

When you have "The Talk." Don't assume. If you feel like you're ready to be exclusive, let them know. Give them the chance to tell you where they are in that way. If they are not at that point, it may just mean they need more time. If they have no desire to get to that point, you need to know that also. Before you move to the next stage, be sure you're on the same page.

WHAT HAPPENS IF IT STARTS GETTING SERIOUS?

By now, you have done the fishing. You have hauled in the catch. As with most things, the end is also the beginning. You've been dating the person for a while. If your goal is to go from single to spouse, it will eventually be time to take things to the next level. It's time to drop the *dating* and be in a relationship. It's time to be exclusive. It doesn't matter who brings up the topic first. After some regular dates, one or both should naturally begin the attachment process.

Regardless of who brings up the topic, the other person is responsible for their own truth about whether they are at the same place emotionally. If you're not there yet, say so; but be clear as to whether or not you wish to eventually get to that stage with them. You may just need more time for your cake to bake.

The idea of attachment can scare off many people, and sometimes gets a bad reputation. As humans, we are wired for connection. In the healthy forms of attachment, emotional connection begins, and the early seeds of intimacy are planted. Healthy attachment is not a sign of weakness; in fact, developing and maintaining secure attachment is a sign of emotional strength. Therefore, communicating and establishing exclusivity within the relationship is significant.

"We believe that every person deserves to experience the benefits of a secure bond. When our partner acts as our secure base and emotional anchor, we derive strength and encouragement to go out into the world and make the most of ourselves. He or she is there to help us become the best person we can be, as we are for them."

—Amir Levine,
Attached: The New Science of Adult
Attachment and How It Can
Help You Find and Keep Love.

Regardless of age, it's okay to use "boyfriend" or "girlfriend". Those feelings at this intimacy stage likely recall the best of youthful love. Regardless of your relational pronouns, saying the word should make you feel a certain way. It's important to clarify the difference between being exclusive and being committed. We will further unpack that difference in the next chapter. This stage is where you begin to seek to deepen the connection and bond between the two of you. This stage requires more investment in nearly every way.

Social Media

If you haven't connected on social media, become friends and follow each other. This is not to spy, but it will give a glimpse into their lives and what they find important. Do they post everything they do and everywhere they go? If so, they will likely want to include you in their feed and timeline. Are you okay with that? Do they only post selfies? If so, could they be really into themselves, or is it PR for their business platform? Self-love is healthy. Love of self is narcissism.

Can you tell by his social media if he has any sense of purpose or vision you could admire? What types of things are they into? What does their social circle look like? They are likely a product of their closest circle of friends. Do they still have pictures of their ex? Are they still attached to or wounded by their past? Do they look single in their timeline? Is it okay with you to see several recent pictures of them and their ex posing for the camera? Do they rant about things you don't care about?

You should not need login access to their social media accounts to gain or keep trust. This would not be a healthy attachment. There should be nothing on social media you need to hide from someone you intend to be exclusive with and develop a deep connection with. Intimacy is the continual journey of revealing deeper parts of your being with someone you care about.

Chivalry

A man's intention to provide a safe and secure space for a woman is evident in his practice of chivalry. It is not dead, and when he is attentive to her needs he silently communicates her value to her. It's not that she can't do things herself like open doors, walk on the curbside of the street or pull out a chair so she can sit down before him.

Royalty is treated like royalty because of its value to the kingdom. The queen is so important in chess because she protects the king. These things have fallen off in our culture, and an older man may not have taught a younger man these things. It is incumbent upon a man to research the topic and extend his hand of service to her regularly, if not throughout the day.

If he expects to be treated like a king, he should act like one by treating her like the royalty most women appreciate. If she openly says she does not like that or she doesn't appreciate it, this may be an indicator of the shared value. He should assume she likes his special treatment and attentiveness until he finds out otherwise. She should make it clear that she notices and appreciates it, if she does. Like most things, the more she openly appreciates what he does, the more likely he'll continue to do it.

If she takes his service and attentiveness for granted, she'll likely find herself reminiscing one day about the things he *used* to do that he doesn't do anymore. If she wants to be treated like royalty, she should be intentional about recognizing and protecting the king when he reveals himself. Most guys crave affirmation from the significant woman in their life. Most good women will reciprocate when their love cup is full to overflowing.

Paying for dates

Paying for dates is less of an issue than initiating dates as opportunities to connect. Both should be intentional during this phase to actively deepen the connection between you two. Dating should not stop because you're now exclusive. The dates just change from *getting to know* to *getting to grow*. The goal is not to fall in love; it is to grow in love. This exclusive relationship is a third entity outside of the two individual people. The relationship is a campfire which both of you are responsible for maintaining. Dating is adding logs to this campfire. We will go deeper into this imagery later.

Don't doubt yourself if you can't afford fancy or expensive dates. There are an infinite number of ways you can plan a fantastic date for little to no cost. Sometimes the simplest dates are the most impactful because they usually involve simplicity, which leaves space for connecting and growth. Think of new and exciting ideas to connect with your partner. Search for at-home or low-cost date ideas. If you have the resources, splurge when possible and do something special to create great memories. Travel in different forms can be a great way to create memories and to see how you both flow through the hustle and details of everything that goes with visiting new places.

Red Flags

The exclusive phase is a great time to focus on one person and gain insight into whether there could be a significant future together. Having this focused time also allows you to be realistic about things that may be red flags to you. Most people in divorce court knew there was a problem when they said "I do" but ignored the red flags.

You must be honest with yourself when things surface; therefore, it is important to be exclusive before being committed. Not having someone in the periphery with whom you went out on a first date last night helps you see the person you're in a relationship with more objectively. At this point, recognizing red flags on the surface will save you from headache and heartache later when you get into real details of the discovery.

Some obvious red flags may include possible addictions, significant and random mood swings, cheating on you, unhealthy and destructive behaviors, a seemingly constant need for drama, an inability to keep a job, constantly talking about and bad-mouthing their ex, signs of attachment issues, men who put down women in general or women who emasculate their man.

The danger here is that if you are not genuinely ready for a relationship, you will find a break-up-worthy fault in anyone. You won't find a 30-year-old car without mileage. Likewise, you won't find a person 30+ years old, single or divorced, with no flaws. If you do, that might be the biggest red flag of them all! They may have indicators of possible red flags, but giving those indicators time to manifest is crucial.

One example could be that you are not intending to be the sole or primary financial provider, yet you've met someone who is unemployed. Give them and yourself time to see if there is a legitimate reason. Maybe they're resetting their career trajectory or just perpetually unemployed.

Another example may be someone with red flags in their past. Have they done the work to address that before meeting you? People can change in many ways when given enough time and hard lessons.

If they have flaws, can they acknowledge them, and are they interested in seriously addressing them? If a true red flag exists and you find that you're not genuinely interested in moving things to deeper levels of intimacy, be honest with yourself and them. Breaking off an early relationship may be awkward, but it's much better than walking down the aisle knowing that you're marrying the wrong person. Allow yourself and them to meet exactly the right person at some point down the road.

Sex

Let's keep this simple:

1. Don't give them anything you don't trust them with before you're ready to trust them with it.
2. You are probably *not* the first person they've done *that* with.
3. Some people use sex as a transaction or use it to keep from attaching emotionally.
4. The "best" sex often comes from the biggest basket cases.
5. If they see you as a trophy, they may lose interest after the trophy is mounted.

PAULA:

Some signs you're getting into the exclusive phase come with really good communication. This is where integrity comes into play. You're having open and honest dialogues with someone and you're not afraid of vulnerability or rejection. That's opening your heart up and being in clear integrity. Saying, "I'm turning off this app now," or "I'm denying other dates and will tell this ex to stop texting me," is being clear.

You should not be exclusive with someone whose actions and words don't match. That's a game and should be a red flag. Alignment with actions and words are important. Stay away from lying and the unavailable person, whether it's time, effort or simply emotional.

JASON:

Are you ready to become exclusive with someone? What are the signs in becoming exclusive? In my experience, it's once you've spent enough time with them. You've either stayed the night with them, been in each other's homes, or maybe you've gone on a trip with them. Things have been going great.

It really comes down to the first fight or the first disagreement. How do you deal with disagreements? How do you communicate if this is your person? If this is the one you see a future with, are you willing and able to work through those disagreements? Have you expressed your boundaries? Are they able to express their boundaries?

I've dealt with "nice guy syndrome", and there's also the "Superwoman syndrome" out there. A lot of guys have been trained to caretake. They don't know how to say no or stand up, and have that backbone a lot of ladies want.

There are many ladies who are very successful when it comes to business. They take care of their household and they want to raise their kids and everything. They may not be able to open up that space of being taken care of, so they need to be aware of who you are, what you want and what you value.

You need to express yourself with clarity and compassion. Always be yourself.

I've seen seemingly great relationships crumble due to no clear communication or good compassionate communication. Are you willing to work with this person and not take it personally when they are triggered or when they're having trouble? Are you able to communicate your needs and wants and boundaries? Are they able to do the same? Is that something you're okay with?

Once, I asked an ex-girlfriend what she wanted out of our relationship—what she wanted from a boyfriend. I just listened to her list of answers. None of them were crazy or outlandish, but I checked in with myself and realized that her answers to me felt like work. They didn't feel like a natural outcropping of something I would want to do. That was the key for me to realize that maybe this wasn't the right person for me. Those answers would not feel like work; they would feel like something I would be willing, able and agreeable to do.

If you're looking to become exclusive and find that, this is the path you want to head down. How do you communicate? How do you handle disagreements? Are you on the same page more than you're not? These are the things you want to look for because these are the building blocks to creating a foundation that will lead you long term into the future.

When you get exclusive with someone, some of the biggest red flags to look for are control issues. If somebody needs to know where you are all the time, if they want to have a joint email or joint bank account to combine all your things together, do you want to go down that road? Those are all control issues and narcissistic red flags.

This is usually an immature or emotionally unavailable person, so they don't trust you. They need to know your whereabouts 24/7 and what you're doing. They get angry if you want to do anything without them. That emotional codependency will not lead to a healthy long term relationship. If you've crossed the threshold into exclusivity and now feel constrained, you'll feel judged and controlled. Those are all red flags which may indicate this person was not honest with you in the dating process. Now you're really starting to see their true colors because actions speak a thousand times louder than words.

Despite what they say, how are they acting? Do you feel free and liberated with this person, or do you feel trapped and controlled? Trust yourself, trust your heart and trust your God. I've had those experiences with people who were great friends of mine. We decided that since we were such great friends, maybe we should date. As soon as we started dating, the wheels came off. We realized we were just great friends and that we needed to stay that way. Trust your gut. Trust your heart. If you're with the right person, you'll feel more free once you're together and exclusive.

GENIE:

Always keep in mind that each human is unique. Unfortunately, we all have an unconscious bias in thinking that what we want is the right thing; therefore, it should also be what they want. If they don't want what we want, something must be wrong with them. It's so logical that I shouldn't have to share it; you should just know it. This causes so many painful problems. This bias will get you into relationship trouble 100% of the time. The truth is that it's just selfishness: *What I want is right; what you want isn't.* Can you see it? Selfishness always destroys relationships.

You need to learn to be explicit in your conversations. You need to explicitly ask for what you want. Let them know what you need. Humans are very bad mind readers. Once you've explicitly asked for what you want, ask if they're willing to deliver it; then talk about what you're willing to do in order to reward the behavior. All of this has to be very explicit, because the interesting thing about men and women is that we were created as opposites—wired from the inside out to be opposites.

Because of that, we think in opposing directions.

The feminine will think emotionally, while the masculine will think logically. He will move to emotion after he goes through logic, and she will move to logic after she goes through emotion. Even if you were the same sex, you're still going to attract your opposite and have to deal with this.

We're talking about masculine energy and feminine energy, which we all have. We have a prime energy in each of us, so because of that, never assume anything in a relationship. Always be very explicit with what you want, what's important to you, and then create partnership. It's not about compromise; it's about creating partnerships. What's important to me is this: What's a deal breaker for me? I want us to be exclusive. That means you won't date anybody else. You'll drop off the dating sites. You won't hang out with old loves. You'll introduce me as your exclusive girlfriend or boyfriend.

Just have the conversation. What does it mean to you? What are you willing to do to make this relationship exclusive? You'll find that every person will have a different answer. That's where it gets a little tough. Every person has their own triggers and wounds, as well as their own unique heart desires; so without having an explicit conversation about it you're going to be wrong 99% of the time.

That's where relationships get really hard, because you assume they think the way you think. But they don't. They actually think in opposing fashions. For instance, women tend to share too much emotion for men to be comfortable, and men tend to share little to no emotion for women to be comfortable. When this happens, a woman will then judge a man as if he's hiding or lying when he shares less emotion than she does. She'll actually have a physical reaction in her body that feels like *Oh, my God. He didn't share everything with me. He must be lying. I need to protect myself from him.*

He's just a man who doesn't share in the way a woman does. You're going to get red flags from all directions when you don't understand that men and women are opposites and process in opposing ways. He's going to get a red flag when she shares too much emotion. He's going to label her as overemotional, when in truth she's just being a woman.

Again, have explicit conversations about what's working, what's not working and what you're willing to do in the partnership to get what you're after. If you find that he or she is lying, that may or may not be one of your dealbreakers. You might mention that you need to rebuild trust with them and explain what's needed in order to do that. It doesn't always mean that you need to walk away, but it always means you need to grow.

Relationships are the crucible of personal development because every relationship will demand that you grow to the next level, no matter how long you've been in the current one. Dealbreakers are unique and personal, and I think it's really important that you know what they are for you. You might even want to sit down and think your way through them.

If something happens, how will you handle it? The purpose is to grow you to the next level, not to run and hide from something that's happening to you. Lying would be a problem, yet we all do it; so how can you use it as a trigger to grow the relationship instead of dumping it? Infidelity would definitely be a red flag, although I have coached many clients through infidelity because it actually happens a lot. There are absolutely ways to get through it and to build a stronger relationship, but it's something you're going to want to pay attention to. Make sure you are able to grow from it.

Hiding from each other, ghosting each other and shutting off from each other are ways to process this. However, if you have an explicit conversation, it might go like this: *Hey, look. You're pulling away and disengaging from me. Do you need time to process? How much time do you need? I'm perfectly willing to give it to you.* Or … *You're just not showing up for me. That's a real problem. We need to find a way to deal with this or I'm out of here.* Finding the tools to deal with all the red flags is the real answer.

Secret #5
Be Committed

Kirk's Q&A

1. What's the difference between being exclusive and being committed?

Exclusive is when you have stopped dating other people and cut yourself off from the singles scene to see if this connection can grow into something long term. Committed is when you've been exclusive for some period, and you are turning the corner of this being a long-term and end-goal relationship. Being committed is like an expired warranty. The maintenance and upkeep are now all on you, as opposed to the manufacturer. It is said that the wine maker is invested, but the grape is committed. Once the wine is made, the grape is all in while the maker moves on to the next grape.

2. What are some indicators that show you are ready to be committed?

You're ready when you've had time to get to know the other person without any other dating or hookups with other people. After you've gotten to know them in the exclusive phase, you will eventually have the chance to see them on good and bad days. You will have opportunity to see how you both resolve conflict. You will see them handle adversity inside and outside of your relationship. Once you see these things and can still envision this person in your life ten years from now, you are probably ready to be committed.

3. What are some signs that show you should pump the brakes on being committed?

You should slow down and hold off on being committed if there are things within your relationship that trigger either one of you. These things could stir up unresolved experiences from your past. Red flags that you're not ready to accept about them for the foreseeable future should give pause to moving to the next level. There's no hurry here, folks! It's okay to take your time. You are under no obligation nor in a rush to take things to the next level. Feel free to grow slowly. I know good chemistry may give a sense of urgency, but rushing could be the worse thing you could do. Enjoy the journey. The journey *is* the destination.

I THINK THIS IS A KEEPER. WHAT DO WE DO?

Now that we've unpacked what it looks like to be exclusive, let's take it to the next level. There is no set amount of time for each phase. What's most important is that both of you are clear about what phase you're currently in. It's not necessary that you both move at the same pace from one level to the next at exactly the same time. It's more that you actively communicate about where each of you is. Being exclusive is a specific phase over some period of time. Being committed is an entirely different phase and time period.

Because you may arrive at this phase at different times, there may be overlap between the two. Each phase does have a beginning and an end, however. The main difference is that the committed phase involves accepting the other person for what you have learned about them thus far. This phase exists at the level of attachment where a forever attachment develops.

This is only *Secret #5*, so we aren't at marriage yet. At this point, though, it's very likely to get to that point. You've already done the self-work prior to dating. You've put yourself out there and have found the catch you were looking for. You've stopped dating other people and focused your intimate attention on this one person. You have observed potential red flags and intentionally decided that, in spite of their imperfections, this is someone you have grown attached to deeply, and they have not displayed deal breakers thus far.

Being exclusive was when you stopped dating others. Being committed begins to look more like seeing the person at their core and desiring that for the foreseeable future. The more you can say yes to the indicators in the below list, the more likely you are to be ready for the committed phase:

1. You are likely in love with this person at some point during the exclusive phase.
2. You truly love the person for who they are. *What* they are is secondary to *who* they are at this point.
3. You regularly remind each other of your love. "I love you" is normally part of saying goodbye when you part company.
4. Your life without them would not have as much meaning.
5. If this person was injured in an accident, you would be at their side as much as feasibly possible.
6. When they hurt, you hurt to some degree.

7. You have developed a Secure attachment to each other and neither one of you doubt it.
8. Given everything you know about them to this point, you want to be with them at least 10 years from now.
9. You can be completely yourself around them and allow them to see your good and bad, light and dark, strengths and weaknesses.
10. You trust them such that you are no longer falling in love; you are growing in love.

Inner Circle

If it hasn't happened yet, you both should be introducing the other person to the closest people in your life. If you have not been introduced to or know anyone else in their life after being in this phase, it may be a huge red flag. An exception to this is if they are a secret government agent or in the Witness Protection Program.

Use caution in allowing this extended circle to overly influence your decision to be in this new relationship. Take their input, though, as they get to know this new person. Sometimes, the people around you can help you see blind spots you may miss. Always consider the source.

If a person in your extended circle cannot keep a healthy relationship or has no stated expertise, you may not want to let them give advice about your own relationship. It could be a red flag, though, if everyone around you gives you the same caution and negative feedback about this person or the relationship. This could be where a relationship or dating coach may benefit you. This person can objectively help keep your head out of the clouds and see things as they are, instead of how you hoped they could be.

Introduce your person to the various social circles in your life. Your party friends may have a different perspective than your spiritual or work circles. Ideally, before the in-person introductions, you will have begun to mention this new person and even share about the progress of your dating journey. If you are introducing them to anyone in your circle, they should already have a good impression of this person because you have been sharing how great he or she is up to this point.

Kids

If you have a regular relationship with your kids, they should get to know this significant other in your life. Kids can be especially challenging. You may want to keep some things in mind. The health of your relationship with your kids can influence how they see this new person coming into your life. Your son or daughter may have some legitimate intuition about this person. At the same time, their unconscious jealousy could provoke them to want to keep new people away. They may act out for attention to be sure they don't lose you to this new person. If you don't have a solid relationship with your kids, they could have any number of motivations to not want you to be in a healthy and intimate relationship.

One example is if your marriage to their other parent ended badly and there was animosity in your split. Kids may have heard negative things about you from their other parent. They may not want you to be happy, the way their other parent may not want you to be happy.

(Note: If your children's other parent talked negatively about you to them, it's likely your ex will have a hard time moving on to a new relationship. Thus, your moving on to a new healthy relationship makes them look more unhealthy or more like a victim. They obviously did not read and follow *Secret #1* in this book!)

Another example is that kids can idolize the notion that you may get back together with their other parent, and someone new could be the reason that cannot happen. There is no age limit to these obstacles with your kids. Older kids could still be against you moving on beyond their other parent. These are just some examples. You should do your best to consider them and their adjustment to this new person in both your lives. They will likely need patience in the process during this committed phase.

If they are younger, start slowly with light and short meetings. Gradually increase the time and the settings.

Women should use caution with the speed of incorporating a new man into the lives of kids. If possible, hold off before leaving your kids alone with or traveling with someone new. There are women and men who have been sexually violated as a child by a new man in their mom's life. I have also heard of extreme cases where men pursue a relationship with a woman to gain access to her kids for the purposes of human trafficking. These are extreme cases, but it can happen.

A new woman in your life may be completely different with you versus with your kids when you're not around. These are not her kids, and the natural maternal bond is not necessarily there. Prior to being unsupervised with your new partner, your kids should be old enough to stand up and advocate for themselves in case a difficult situation arises. Rushing the process with kids can adversely impact the long-term relationship with this potential stepparent.

How this person treats your kids is an indicator of how compatible this person is for you. It's also an indication of how they feel about you. Your new partner should be concerned about your relationship with your kids and seek to foster a better relationship between you and them however possible.

If you have kids and your partner does not, they may not be aware of the parent-child dynamic. In this case, mutual grace may be required to sort out all sides. Your ex should not dictate the limits and structure of your current relationship simply because you share custody of the kids with them. Honor your parenting commitments first and give the appropriate amount of time for the new relationship to fold into that role.

(Note: If your kids are the reason you cannot move into the committed phase, you may want to start back at *Secret #1*. Consider whether you should even be dating for a spouse. If this is the case, maybe you need to remain completely single until all of your kids are adults. For people with Avoidant attachment styles, kids can be a typical excuse to break off relationships.)

Family & Friends

It's important for your family and friends to meet this new person, as well. To the degree you are close to your parents, siblings and extended family, gradually incorporate your new relationship into conversations. In some cases, family can have motivations and biases that oppose this new relationship. Hopefully, the adults around you have matured and want to see you happy and in a healthy relationship. Give them permission to point out potential red flags, or at least indicators to watch out for. Many friends have found themselves supportive in helping someone get through a difficult breakup, while also admitting they saw warning signs but did not mention them.

Oxytocin is a great drug, and it's what chemically and intimately binds us as humans. One of its side effects, though, is emotional blindness in new relationships. True friends don't let friends date while drunk on Oxytocin.

Remember That Love Letter?

That love letter wasn't suggested without a reason. There's a method to the madness!

You have made your way through this journey over whatever period of time. You have done your self-work. You have searched for and tossed back all the fish in your net that you were not trying to catch. You may have made some bad choices and hopefully learned some lessons along the way. You may have thought you were close, only to have a rug pulled from under you. You may have been tempted to quit more than once and just be alone forever.

Finally, you found someone who seemed promising in the early stages. Time has revealed greater things about them. You both stopped dating others. Healthy attachment began to form between the two of you. You became "official". Maybe your family and kids have had the opportunity to meet them.

Now … Pull out that letter and read it to yourself when you're alone. Is it that person? Again, do not tell them about the letter or let them read it. This letter is only for your future spouse. Hopefully, you would have recognized by now if this person was not a good fit for you, since you know yourself very well.

If the person you are with now is nothing like the person you wrote to in the letter, you may want to proceed from here with caution. Maybe even consider what is different. Are there one or two things that don't line up, or did you write to a completely different person? This is gut check time and requires personal honesty and integrity. If there is no real overlap in who you wrote to and who you are with, this may be one of the biggest red flags of all. Are you settling? Are you in a dysfunctional, yet passionate, relationship? Is your connection based on trauma bonding?

The intent here is not to give you cold feet or an excuse to give in to fear and run. If you were a runner, you would not have likely made it this far on the journey. This is about keeping true to the goal and process in this book. Things only get more serious with higher levels of consequences from here. You may be better off reevaluating things now, rather than experiencing a situation later that may be harder to walk away from. Ending things here may be tough, but it would be a lot easier now than beyond this point.

PAULA:

Commitment is like combining assets and other things that would need to be formally and legally undone. Here you begin to co-mix and co-mingle serious parts of your life. Signs of someone worth committing to are:

- There is calmness in communication when there are hiccups to deal with. We're all human, it's normal and natural. There's a definable calmness and communication when you're not being called names.
- You're not being put down; you're being amplified, uplifted, valued and respected.
- They are emotionally mature. If something comes up, they know how to handle it objectively.
- You amplify and uplift each other. There's no need to put someone down just to make the other feel better.
- There's a polarity—a connection—between you two. Even if something goes awry for a while, they come back again. This is the dance.

A fear of commitment could exist. Many of us didn't grow up with really good influences on how to do relationships and commitment. There's probably much fear of commitment out there because we hear *Do this. How do we make this work?* The thing to remember is that we make our own decisions and are responsible for ourselves. In other cultures, partners are much more open-hearted. Being vulnerable is just normal.

Westerners seem to be very closed off. It's interesting, because we're all dying for connection. It's what we actually want. Things are easy and simple in some ways, but deep dives in others. Dance with each other and have fun playing together. Don't put people on pedestals. We're all human, and we have our stuff to deal with at times. That only invites us to go deeper if we're willing to.

JASON:

If you're moving from exclusive to committed, you've done your homework. You've been with this person exclusively. We're not seeing the red flags. We're not seeing control issues. Once you get to that place, commitment now becomes your thing. If you came from an unhealthy relationship, you are now attempting to have a healthy one. You've committed to being exclusive with this person. It feels like all the boxes have been checked. Not that you actually have a list, but you definitely want to make sure they are fitting with you.

Once you get into that committed space, our past

traumas might sometimes hold us back emotionally. By dealing with them and your unconscious stories, you can communicate that with your person so they understand. "I'm committed to you. I think you're my person. Here's what gives me anxiety. Here's what I'm worried about. Here's what I've dealt with in the past."

Give them the space to express their stuff, too. If you've been holding anything back, this is the time to express it. This is the person you're building with. You do not want to leave trapdoors for them to fall through because you didn't express past traumas or anxieties. This is almost your last chance to vet them.

I think when it comes to moving from exclusive to committed, it's almost like you have to turn that focus back on yourself. "Okay, here's what's going on with me. I haven't had emotionally intelligent, intimate relationships in the past, and we're moving in that direction. I need to open the door and tell you I'm freaking out so you can tell me if you're freaking out."

Have those conversations in an open way and allow yourself to be open-minded and open-hearted. Keep your eyes open and don't fall into the fears of past anxieties and traumas. When you go from exclusive to committed, it can seem like there's a huge mountain or barrier you now have to cross. It's really just a step in communication, openness and honesty.

I've seen people pull away from being committed because they had to suddenly be intimate with the other person. They had to be vulnerable in a way they'd never done before. If they would look at the other person for who they are and not allow past stories and anxieties to taint the story in their head, they might actually be able to step in and have a conversation about it.

By allowing the other person to speak their truth, you'll have transparency and vulnerability with each other. That's where commitment comes in. Maybe this is the one who will accept you, understand you, work with you and listen to your anxieties, traumas and fears. They will want to work with you through all of that. If you show them all your scars and wounds, let them judge for themselves if they think you're the one.

Commitment means opening your heart and making yourself vulnerable in the most intimate way. That's a huge leap for anyone. Are you willing to be that person who leads the way? Show that to them.

I think commitment is scary for most people because most of our traumas and anxieties came from our families. Those who were supposed to be our most intimate and loving examples were the ones who caused the most damage. Past experiences have shown that those we thought were supposed to be the most loving and committed were the ones who did the most damage.

It's terrifying for most of us to drop the façade and the armor to expose our hearts. We're showing someone who we really are and allowing ourselves to be vulnerable. They now have all that ammunition to use against us and we are completely naked. Opening yourself up is one of the most terrifying things because you don't know how this person is going to use that against you. They could cut out your heart, but you trust them not to. Learning to trust another person with your most vulnerable secrets can be the most terrifying part about being committed.

GENIE:

To me, commitment in marriage is *til death do us part*. That doesn't mean we have to live through hell until one of us dies, though. It means I'm not going anywhere when things get rough (and they always will because it's part of life), and that I'm committed to solving every issue that comes along. That's what it means to me, personally; however, marriage and dating are two different things.

A dating commitment might mean I'm dedicated to finding out if this will work for a lifelong partnership; so that means I'm willing to do the work that it may take to create a partnership, which makes us both better. I would be really concerned with someone who thought that just because they found "the one" there would be no problems. *Oh, the perfect person entered my life, so now everything will be perfect!* There is no such thing.

Relationships are designed to grow you, and it will often be difficult in order to take you to your next level of growth. *Where do I need to grow?* That's one of the things I coach through with my clients who are really struggling with that behavior. Where do you need to grow so you can get to the next level and find greatness?

Commitment

I honestly don't think people are afraid of commitment as much as they are about making a commitment. That's very important to understand—what are you each willing to commit to? Make sure you have conversations in the dating phase about what you would like to bring to the relationship and what you would like to receive from the other person. From that space, you can begin to ask what you're willing to give and receive from each other. Those are important things to talk about.

If it brings you great joy to cook a big meal in the morning, but your partner wants to go work out on an empty stomach, you've got a real challenge and you're going to have to work your way through it.

That may not a dealbreaker, but it could be annoying because it hasn't been talked about.

I had a client who told me he was about to marry his fiancée. He said he had a real problem because he wanted her to be the one to initiate sex most of the time. She wasn't willing to initiate most of the time, but she did from time to time. The issue came down to what it really meant to him. He felt "less than" as a man if she didn't initiate, so that was an issue with him. We worked on other ways she'd be willing to show him what a great man he was to her.

You need to get really clear on what you want, what it does for you, and what the other person is willing to deliver for you. We are typically the answer to most of our own problems. One person walking in love can solve anything. If you walk in love, it usually solves everything, even if it's love for yourself. Love is what's required to make a relationship work; without it, no relationship will work.

I don't care if you're the perfect fit for each other without love, it's not going to work because we require love to live. If we feel like we're not getting it because it's being delivered in the wrong manner, we will walk away. We might disengage. We might cheat. We might lie. We might hide. We might fight, but we're going to do something to make sure that love is there. Be explicit. This is the love I want to give. This is the love I want to receive. You'll get there. Most people don't do that work. They expect the other person to come up with the right recipe for what makes you feel loved, and they expect they'll do it through mind reading. That makes relationships impossibly hard and painful.

Good Traits to Look For

As a keeper, they would have to show a deep caring for your desires and needs. Keep in mind that desires are one thing and needs are another. To create the best and healthiest relationships, you need to create intimacy, and that means you have to understand the other person. You must understand what their needs are.

I'll refer back to men and women as opposites. You will attract your opposite 100% of the time. It's the opposing natures and energies that create the attraction and passion. As opposites, that means their needs will *not* be your needs, so they never occur to you because you need something different. Understanding what their needs are is a great sign of love and commitment. Be willing to deliver it, or at least talk about it. Another sign of love and commitment is understanding and being curious about the other person.

I have another couple as clients. She is very emotional, and he is very stoic. Opposites attract, right?

When she's having a very emotional reaction, he's very loving and caring. It's exactly what she needs. He's aware that he needs to stay even-keeled while she's being emotional instead of making her wrong for feeling those emotions. That creates a sense of peace in her that she didn't have access to before. It's absolutely fascinating.

Always keep in mind that we're opposites, and it's by design. Being opposites can create the greatest and highest levels of passion. If you try to make the other person like you, it could actually kill a lot of the passion in the relationship. Reach for curiosity and understanding without judgment. Be curious. Be understanding or create understanding, then be nonjudgmental. Those are great signs of a long-term, very healthy relationship. Remember, these relationship skills have to be learned and cultivated, because nobody hits the planet already knowing them.

Secret #6
Discovery

Kirk's Q&A

1. **How do you approach the discovery process with your mate?**

With guts! The discovery process is likely to be uncomfortable for all. The things we are most challenged and embarrassed by are revealed during this phase. You are literally showing all your cards and giving full inventory of who and what your life has become to this point. The good, the bad, and surely the ugly will be known by your partner. No one said intimacy is always fun or comfortable. This is critical to have the full picture of what you are committing to for the long term.

If you don't trust this person with every detail of your life, you may not be ready; or this may not be a trustworthy person. Some of what they are about to find out could be embarrassing if posted on social media. Do you trust them with that?

2. What are 5 common dealbreakers that could tank a relationship?
   1. Porn addiction
   2. Cheating
   3. Substance abuse
   4. Unforgiveness
   5. Physical/emotional/mental abuse

3. How do you deal with a dealbreaker?
You must make the personal choice of whether or not this is something you can live with indefinitely. Some things that may be a deal-breaker can be addressed or corrected. Just because it's a dealbreaker now doesn't mean you should walk away now.

4. What are some signs that you may need to walk away?
The dealbreaker cannot be corrected, or the person is not willing to address it for the sake of the relationship. Walking away before you get physically, legally or financially intertwined with the person is easier than afterwards.

5. Are your mutual future goals in alignment?
It's important to consider whether the two of you want the same things in life. What picture would you individually paint about what your life would look

like together 30 years from now? Are those pictures similar or identical? If you fundamentally want different things in life, you will forever be going in two different directions.

HOW CAN I BE SURE THEIR BAGGAGE DOESN'T BECOME MY LUGGAGE?

Now it's time for things to get real. There is no set timetable for how quickly a couple moves through these phases and Secrets. Some may meet the person of their dreams and move lightning fast to this point. In my opinion, it is the *exception*, not the rule, when a couple breezes their way through these steps in a short amount of time AND goes on to have a successful, healthy long-term relationship.

In most instances these days, it takes time to sort out all the intricacies and complexities within a relationship to have a successful marriage. In any case, by the time you get to the doorsteps of whatever venue to say "I do," you should know all about the person to whom you are saying "I do." This Secret is more technical and practical than anything else. At this point, you have (or are preparing to) possibly put a ring on it. It is time to fully pull back the curtains and expose everything so that there are no surprises once the relationship is legally binding.

The discovery process may be the most uncomfortable and vulnerable step in many ways. I am intentional about using the term "discovery" here. By legal definition, discovery is when you exchange information about all the facts of the case. This may involve revealing the most shameful or unattractive details of your life. You owe it to each other to reveal everything prior to taking the last step into an actual forever relationship. If you are not ready or willing to do this, you are definitely not ready for marriage.

You might consider giving your relationship more time to develop the level of intimacy it takes to bare all of your good and bad with this person. There's no hurry. Take your time. Get there when each of you are ready. That may be two different timelines. Ideally, and at this point, there should be little to no judgment between you two. You should be able to accept every part of who they are. If you cannot commit to all of them, you should not be marrying them.

These examples of topics to be revealed or discussed during discovery are not necessarily all-encompassing. These are generally the main things that can cause major issues if they surface after marriage. If you cover these areas, any other topics you wish to bring up or explore should be a piece of cake.

"When you're entering into a business partnership, you do your homework. Disclose all relevant financial information and discuss shared goals and

visions to make every effort to be successful in that business. Just as laws apply to a business formation, they also apply to a marriage, which are not usually realized until the divorce. So why wouldn't you approach a personal relationship with the same care?

Exchanging financial information (income, debts, assets), discussing your perspectives on money (savings, retirements, monthly expenses, extraordinary expenses, etc) and planning goals together is imperative in having a successful marriage. You can either informally agree on shared goals or you can discuss with an attorney whether a premarital agreement (a legally binding agreement) would be better for your particular situation."

—Teresa M. Wilkins, Esquire,
Law Firm of Teresa Wilkins, LLC

Finances

Along with addictions and infidelity, money is one of the main reasons marriages fail. You should have a detailed discussion about each of your incomes and expenses. Plan a time for a formal discussion on your budgets. You may discover that one or both of you have differing views on keeping budgets and how (or if) each of you track the flow of money in and out of your bank accounts. Hopefully, you spent some time in *Secret #1* getting your financial affairs in order. If not, do so by the time you cross this bridge.

This may be a reason to delay getting married. It is best to bring little to no financial baggage into a marriage. Share tax returns and possibly bank statements for the past year. If any part of their income comes from a former spouse through spousal support, consider how that may change after you get married in this relationship. If they're paying child support, when does that end, and how will it impact your finances going forward?

This is a fantastic time to discuss how the two of you would agree to handle mutual or combined finances once married. Will you keep separate accounts or combine everything into one? Could it be a combination of both? Who would be responsible for paying shared household expenses, and how will money be managed together? Are there any financial goals you would like to set together? This could include property.

In whose home would you live? Would you sell the other home or rent it? Are there other investment properties? Do you have a financial retirement plan or any savings? Are there life insurance policies, and who would be listed as the beneficiaries? What health and medical benefits do each of you have? A certified financial planner may be able to help walk through these and other questions relative to your personal and combined finances.

Credit

Similar to getting clarity on finances, knowing each of your financial credit scores and histories can save loads of undue stress and heartache if known up front. Pull both credit reports. Beyond just credit score, discuss individual debt and anything currently pending. Being informed of what you are partnering with credit-wise will allow you to be better informed of what your prospects are for joint ventures, like purchasing a home or a vehicle.

This likely came up during the discovery of income and expenses; however, just because they are paying a debt doesn't mean the debt does not or will not exist in the near future. Adverse credit or lack of financial stability may or may not be a dealbreaker in the relationship. Finding out after getting married can make someone feel like they were tricked into something they didn't agree to. I will quickly throw in here that criminal records are similar to credit history and should be discussed. Both can impose limitations on the relationship in the foreseeable future.

Medical

Your physical health is important to your soon-to-be spouse. There should be no surprises with how many miles remaining this ride is likely to have. When is the last time either of you had a physical? Commonly, women are more in tune with their health than men. A lot of men stay as far away from doctors as possible. Hopefully, you both can get a good understanding of any current or past family medical history. Do you have any health goals? Are you on any medications? I know this sounds like a medical questionnaire, but there's a reason your doctor wants to know as much as possible about you prior to taking you on as a new patient. This may sound strange, but both of you should take an STI/STD screening prior to marriage. Whether you've already been sexually active together or are both virgins, starting with a clean slate of understanding will bring peace of mind.

Prenup?

Given everything discussed above, you may consider a prenuptial (or premarital) agreement. It might sound strange to go this far, only to bring up a legal agreement for what happens if the marriage dissolves. All marriages end. In the best-case scenario, the marriage ends when *death do us part*. Anyone who has ever been divorced has learned that a marriage is a legal agreement to combine assets and liabilities. The divorce is a legal dissolution of those tangible things.

Even when a spouse dies, their assets and liabilities are legally transferred to someone else. That someone else is commonly the surviving spouse. Hopefully, there's a legal will in place to further establish the distribution of those things in addition to the established laws in each state.

A prenup may be considered a will prior to marriage for everything that existed prior to or acquired during the marriage. Besides premarital debt and assets, one example may be intellectual property, such as rights to anything published prior to the marriage. If you want that to go to your spouse or kids from a previous relationship, those are things that should be spelled out to help avoid confusion or civil lawsuits after the marriage ends. The most obvious place to start with this discussion is hiring an attorney specializing in this field. Since you have had the discussion regarding finances, debt, etc, you are already prepared to lay everything out with an attorney to help decide if this may be appropriate.

Religion

This can likely be a straightforward discussion. If you have gotten this far, this topic shouldn't be a surprise. It is something worth covering, though. Quite simply, what are your individual spiritual beliefs, if any? Do you have a desire to practice any faith or religion together? What are your thoughts around financially supporting a church or spiritual organization? In what type of venue or setting would you like to get married? What would each of you prefer that wedding to look like, if there is any type of ceremony at all?

Being able to have these in-depth and transparent discussions is vital before becoming spouses. This will help you both be better prepared for what to expect once you two are married. These discussions may also cause you to pause and rethink if this is the right person for you or if a deal-breaker exists based on your realistic priorities.

You owe it to the other person to know everything and come to their own conclusions as to whether you are the right person for them. Being honest with yourself regarding what is acceptable for you or not will help guard against regrets down the road. If you have successfully navigated these discussions and have decided to stay together for the long haul, then you are ready to move on to the last Secret.

"It doesn't matter so much what page you're on, as long as you're both on the same page."

—**Kirk**

PAULA:

I'm gonna say this as gently as I can. There are always going to be land mines. To be clear, I have a zero abuse zone. I think everybody should have a zero abuse zone. That doesn't mean there aren't going to be other things. I was dating a guy once, and I found out three months into it that he had two kids instead of one. These are things that should not be a surprise after a certain point.

I'm always going to be on a path of growth and self-discovery; that's part of the dance. You're never *not* going to be hurt by somebody. It's just not possible. You'll also be okay 100% of the time. We all have a range. To me, that range is what creates the beauty of humans. Find someone who you want to dance with in that range. You can build and grow anything with that.

JASON:

If you haven't already dug through all your dirt, we definitely want to make sure this person is emotionally compatible with you. Is your crazy compatible with their crazy? Is your past stuff compatible? Are you both working on healing? Do they have the same core values as you? Do you know who they voted for? Do you know what they do during the holidays? Do you know what they're passionate about? You've probably discovered most of these things before you got to this stage, but maybe it's time to dig in.

Maybe you need to see if you're both really committed. Do they need to know all of your dirty laundry little secrets from past relationships? People attach to certain mental things that they may not even be aware of, but if you can't let go of the past, it's very hard to move toward the future and live in the present.

Did you have the conversation where you expose all your stuff and both agree to let it go? Are you on the same page financially about the kids? Are you on the same page on whether or not you want to join everything together or keep things separate?

Okay, we're getting ready to sign these contracts. We're committing ourselves to each other. What's the fine print? Are you in alignment or in harmony with something you can work on and tolerate? Are you connecting with someone with whom you can build, or are you just settling? Don't settle. Don't tolerate. Make sure this person is someone you're committing to if you're thinking about marriage or moving in together. Are you both looking to grow together?

Make sure you're covering all the little things. They'll want you to be transparent and have conversations. Some of those conversations may irritate you, but with the right person they will become the glue that holds you together.

GENIE:
I've discovered that the number one problem in relationships is the lack of understanding of how

opposite we truly are. When I encounter a troubled relationship, I teach men how women work. Then I teach women how men work, because with that basic understanding you can solve 99.9% of problems ahead of time. I actually spend most of my coaching time there because I believe it solves most problems.

When you begin to understand how a man works versus how a woman works, you stop judging each other as being wrong. You stop trying to fix your partner, which is very painful for all of us. You stop trying to make them cancel behaviors just so you can feel better. Women are not wrong for being emotional and processing emotions. Men are not wrong for processing with logic and reacting visually to sexual cues (which women typically do not).

If you take the wrongness and judgment out of a relationship, you're left with *Wow, I understand you now!* This will work better for you, and it solves most of the problems. You can't create intimacy without understanding. If you judge the other person wrongly, you can't create partnership. If you separate the problem from the person, you can solve the problem without making a person wrong.

I do most of the discovery work in the very beginning of a relationship. The quicker you do it, the less heartache you go through. If you talk about your personal struggles and what you really want at the beginning, you'll quickly sort through the wrong partners. You won't walk away with a bunch of wounds from your dating and relationship experiences that someone else has to fix. That takes great growth.

Questions Before Marriage

- Do you want to get married? If so, how long before you want to?
- Do you want kids?
- Are you open to my kids?
- Would you expect to have control over how I raise my kids?
- Do you want to work full time?
- Do you want to be taken care of and stay home to raise kids?
- What are your dreams?
- What would your retirement look like?
- Is religion important to you?
- What do you think of family or your ex?
- How do you handle family relationships?
- How important is your mom or your dad to you?
- What do you think about your siblings?
- What kind of a family would you like to build, and how would you build it?
- What do you love spending your time doing?
- Would you have a problem if I go on adventures while you stay in a hotel and read a book?

- Would you feel abandoned as I go out on my adventure?

I had another client couple. He loved base jumping, but she didn't even know what that was. She didn't even like the outdoors. As we worked through this, she actually went base jumping with him. She got to the point where she was willing to give it a try, and ultimately discovered that her preference was to stay at the camp and wait for him. When he returned, it was better for him without the pressure of asking her to go. It's not that you want everything to be the same. It's about what you're willing to do or give to each other.

The quicker you find out the information, the better your relationship will be. That means you have to be real, open and honest as you get to know each other. When dating, we usually try hard to present the best of ourselves. That's great, but try to present the whole picture of who you are—the good, the bad and the ugly. Share your rotten day and how you handle stress to see if they can handle you on those days, which will come. You want to find a partner who can handle you in those times.

Secret #7
Go All In

Kirk Q&A

All-In Questions

1. If their financial situation completely changed, would you be all-in?
2. If they became confined to a wheelchair, would you be all-in?
3. If their physical appearance changed drastically, would you be all-in?
4. If they got a terminal disease, would you be all-in?
5. If your kids/family did not like them, would you be all-in?
6. Are you on the same page with the roles and division of labor within the relationship?

WE'RE ABOUT TO SAY "I DO." GOT ANY ADVICE?

This book is for those hoping to get from single to spouse. If you've gotten this far, there's one thing you must understand and accept:

Marriage is 50/50.

WRONG!!!

Marriage destined for divorce is 50/50!

A marriage destined for long term success is not 50/50; it is 100/100. It is two complete beings coming together to multiply and amplify one another. This results in being greater together than you are apart. Statistically, most marriages end in divorce. This is because, in today's culture, two incomplete people often come together and expect the other to meet them in the middle. When you multiply fractions, you get a fraction. Expecting the other to come halfway implies you have intention to only go so far in your effort to be what you need to be in the marriage.

The process of legally dissolving a marriage quickly reveals how much of a percentage each person has (or had) in the marriage. Dissolution is division. Division of assets, debts, parenting time, property, peace and happiness. Rarely does anyone come out whole from the divorce process, or as whole as they were prior to divorce. Usually, the only participants that come out better are the attorneys. Huge legal bills normally indicate one or both parties in the divorce attempted to come out of the divorce with as much of the fraction as possible.

There is such an emphasis on divorce here because relational forensics can often point back to the couple entering the wrong marriage or at the wrong time. As an engagement begins long before a ring goes on any finger, so too does a couple's divorce begin long before there is a petitioner and a respondent. If both are not ready to be 100/100, you should not get married. Maybe you would be better suited maintaining separate finances, homes or lives until both are ready … if ever. Many people choose to be in relationship without getting married or wait however long it takes for both people to be all-in.

The Campfire

Picture a marriage like a campfire. If you've ever tried to start a fire from scratch, you've experienced feeling frustrated or you developed the patience required to create something from nothing. First, you must ensure the environment is right to not only light, but maintain the fire after it's lit. Not only do you first need the tools to start it, but you also need the fuel to maintain it.

Normally, the fire starts with a spark meeting fuel. Once there's an ignition of the small ingredients, you must fan the smoke until a flame comes alive. The initial flame is small. Throwing on a huge log immediately will kill the kindling's flame. This is where patience and steady work pays off. This fire is a living thing. It eats, breathes and moves. It starts young and small, but with proper nurturing it can grow into something healthy and beneficial to all. The out-of-control fire can destroy everything around it; but properly cared for, it can provide heat for safety and cooking.

This campfire represents the third entity in your relationship. It's neither one of you, specifically, rather something living you both must work on and maintain. If there's a problem with the fire, it's not as much as reflection of the other person as it is the work being put into maintaining the fire.

Focus on the fire in times of trouble. What does the fire need? Both of you must be 100% committed to the fire. You must both feed the fire either at the same time or more likely in your own way when it needs it. The fire may have been primarily started by one of you. If only one of you is feeding the fire, that person will eventually run out of logs to add. You cannot just be consumers of the fire, but also must be willing to be its creators and curators.

The fire also needs to be stirred up by turning

the burning logs to reveal fresh fuel already there. When you wake up in the morning and throughout the day, you must be aware of the condition of the fire and what it needs at that moment. *What can I do to feed the fire right now?* This is the mentality you should have. If this sounds like something you cannot accept, maybe it's not the right time or the right person for marriage. When there is an argument or disagreement, regardless of who was in the wrong, both must be willing to be part of the solution.

"When I work with a couple in crisis where one person has an addiction (to pornography for example), I say the problem is his/hers, but the solution is both of theirs. This is because the solution is intimacy, and if both don't desire getting to that point, there's no hope."
—**Kirk**

When both people are committed to the fire, the couple finds themselves mutually serving one another. Both are whole and responsible for self and yes, both can be more whole with an intimate partner covering weaknesses while amplifying strengths. This is not a linear concept, meaning it's not directional. It is circular, as in flow within the relationship. Both learn to give as they receive. The best giver is a good receiver.

In the context of a truly intimate relationship, the two become intertwined. As you give and serve the other, you experience the flow coming back to you. You realize eventually that you are not giving, you are returning. You both give so that their cup overflows and you receive from their saucer. This is receiving from their resource, not their source. You receive from their saucer into your cup. Your cup overflows to your saucer where they receive from.

Flow is natural. It is not forced. There's no need for scorekeeping. There's no pressure, like water through pipes. This mutual service in its highest form becomes safe, secure, mutual submission. Most people have problems with the concept of submission because they have not experienced submission that results from giving.

It is best for both to maintain a sense of self, even within mutual service and submission of an intimate relationship. This diagram represents maintaining a part of your identity while intertwining self with each other.

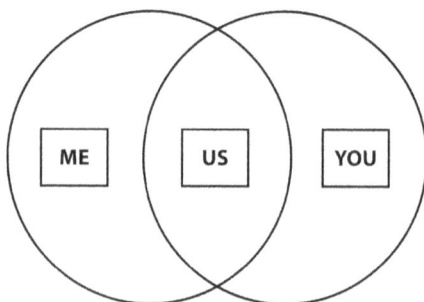

PAULA:

I think a lot of people can get lost in each other in a relationship. You don't want to start resenting people. Clear your communication or be clear in what you desire. Respect each other. Have time together to have fun. Do your own stuff, too, and be your own person.

JASON:

You will be astonished at how easy it is, how things just work, and how clear and concise communication is. These are the things to focus on. If you're going all-in with somebody and you're committed and ready to spend your life together keep focus on the positives. Keep focus on the joy and the love. Remind each other what you love about the other. Learn to laugh as much as possible. Don't avoid conflict or the hard conversations.

If you've come this far and you're ready to go all in, it's those previous hard conversations and wading through the muck that got you here. Embrace them, and don't view them as trials or tribulations. Once you appreciate that, stay focused on the process because many in society already focus on the negative. It takes far less energy to focus on the positive. It takes fewer muscles to smile than to frown. These things will keep you not only committed, but in love and growing together.

Those I have talked with who have successfully committed and are in long term relationships tell me about how their partners' faults, foibles and idiosyncrasies are the things they love most. They're the little things only they know that make them feel special about the relationship. If they hadn't gotten vulnerable and created that deep intimacy, they never would have learned about all those little foibles they know, love and cherish.

We've forgotten how to be transparent and share. We've all been taught to edit instead of just sharing what's on our mind. If you share something that's bothering you, you may find out you had it all wrong. Maybe now you can laugh about it. Maybe you judged wrongly and just made up a story in your head. Learning to express yourself and laugh about these things is a great way to create the glue and the epoxy that will hold you together in the long run. You're a team now, not just one person. This thing together is creating energy, and that's what's going to carry you both forward.

GENIE:

When you enter into an all-in relationship, whether or not you get married, remember that you also enter into it with their family. Let me put it this way: When my kids were growing up and it became time for them to date, I made sure to create my own relationship with the person who was interested in dating my child. Now that they are married, I make sure I have my own unique relationship with my sons-in-law and daughter-in-law. They are family, so I make sure to reach out to them. I build that relationship consciously and intentionally.

I think that's an amazing sign of a well-rounded partner who's willing to enter into all my relationships to create genuine relationships with them. I would talk through what "all in" means to me and what it means to the other person. Nobody gets to determine what "all in" means except you. When you know, share it explicitly and figure out if that's enough or if something more is needed from the other person.

You're creating a partnership where two whole people come together to build something much better than they could have made on their own. You won't know what the "much better" is until you have an explicit conversation about it; then, together you create whatever that life is. Expect challenges in your relationship. Hard times are necessary to help us grow. It doesn't mean either of you are bad people. Just go to the next level and walk in love with another human being. Love is the most powerful force on the planet.

If you want to have a magnificent life, you are required to grow by loving yourself and others at all times. There's no goal post; you will always continue to grow. It's about creating a deeper understanding about yourself and the other person so you can deliver love on higher levels. There will always be more love. If you learn how to give and receive more of it, you will have a magnificent life.

Seven Tips
1. Make the other person's needs important to you.
2. Never judge; only get curious.
3. When things get difficult, use joy as a tool to cut the pressure and move through it.
4. When you encounter a problem, always ask yourself where you need to grow first.
5. Give each other room to be without each other. Freedom creates fabulous relationships.
6. Learn your partner's love language, then communicate with it daily—especially when you don't want to.
7. Ask for what you need, and receive what they are willing to give.

CONCLUSION

PAULA:
Enjoy the process and the journey and don't put too much pressure on yourself. Just have fun with it and be *you*. Enjoy life as it is right now, whether you're

partnered or not. Enjoy it, enjoy it, enjoy it … boom shakalaka!

JASON:

In closing, I would say you're not perfect. Get comfortable with imperfection because perfectionism is a lie. Find joy in the little things because those are what you'll remember as you move forward. Are you perfect for the person you're with, and are they perfect for you? You probably can't be perfect together. Life is messy. Emotions are messy. The world is messy. Can you find the person who's messy with you? Find comfort in the messiness. Go out there and make a mess as a person. Make a mess together and enjoy life in a messy way. That's my best advice.

GENIE:

Men want and need to be honored and appreciated for being a man—not for what he delivers to you, because it usually won't be delivered in the way a woman wants to receive it. Conversely, women want and need to be feminine and emotional with their men and not be judged wrongly for it. Allow her to be a woman. A client once said this to me: "Genie, you mean to tell me that my job is to protect her ability to feel things and to feel them deeply?" It's one of my favorite quotes. It's a man's job to make it safe for a woman to feel deeply whenever she wants.

Women process life through emotion, so they

need to be able to feel, to feel like she's in a very safe place. There is a safety that only men can deliver to women, and it's an amazing gift. I must say that most women don't feel safe in expressing their emotions in the presence of men. Often, they are cut off, "fixed", or told to think about something else. This is very painful for women; but the more emotion she can feel (yes, even negative emotions), the more light and passion she'll bring to his life.

The more honor and appreciation a man feels from a woman, the more strength and safety he'll bring to her life. Accept and appreciate the differences between the sexes. We are the greatest gift to each other. Love is the greatest force on the planet, and it's what makes life worth living. Your journey of giving and receiving love is the most fulfilling and meaningful part of your life. Never give up on love. Keep giving it and never stop receiving it, and it will make your life magnificent. One person walking in love can transform anything. Love solves everything.

KIRK:

Hopefully, you have followed the best path for you to get from single to spouse. As mentioned previously, the end is normally the beginning. Ideally, you find yourself in the most fulfilling, intimate and unconditionally connected relationship possible. Once you cross the finish line of marriage, you discover a whole new race to be run. This race involves a deeply committed partner who is willing to lead and follow through all the ups and downs of the course laid out in front you two.

Secrets #3–#7 of this book still apply after being in a long-term relationship and marriage. There are many roads to the same destination, and most paths can look completely different from others, even when they go in the same direction. Modern dating can be tricky and downright complicated. Be patient. Be persistent. Forgive quickly. Give yourself grace to enjoy the journey. This may involve learning from your mistakes and hitting the reset button at times. You never fail if you learned something in the process. The only true path is the one that works best for you.

We have offered you a general path based on our experience, both personal and professional. Hopefully, you can learn from our mistakes and observations. We invite you to join us and allow us to join you in your journey. We are real people, and hope to be in touch with you in your challenges and triumphs.

To the men in particular, I would like to partner with you. Often, we can be stuck between the blue pill performance and the rebellion expected in red pill thinking. I believe there's a space in between. When we are sure of who we are and what we are meant to do, this brings clarity in *why* we want to date or be in a healthy relationship. I would like to help you in your journey toward clear-pill thinking in terms of your purpose, dating or relationship journey.

I encourage both men and women to engage with me and this team of superheroes. Connect with us on social media. Contact us directly and let us know your thoughts and experience. Share with us the things you agree or disagree with in this book. Allow us to help you do things differently than the status quo. Allow us to help you be a part of the new way to date in the modern age.

Additional Resources

Did you know that sex is *only* 1 of the 40 ways to connect in a relationship?

40 FORMS OF
INTIMACY
Integrating Daily Connection Into
Your Couple Relationship

ALEX A. AVILA

This book contains 40 mini-chapters with 200+ exercises to help you create and fully enjoy a safe, intimate relationship!

Whether single or in a relationship, learn powerful relationship principles and practical techniques from a licensed professional counselor and certified sex and couples therapist!

Book available on Amazon!

~~~~~~

Intimate Foundations
Online Relationship Course

What we ALL wish we knew growing up!

✓ Understand lifelong patterns
✓ Communicate clearly and effectively
✓ Navigate personality differences with skill and respect
✓ Discover new ways to intimately connect that last! *...and much more!*

Designed and facilitated by

RELATIONSHIP INSTITUTE OF THE ROCKIES

Alex A. Avila
MA, LPC, CSAT, CST, CPTT, ACS, NCC, CAT, CBCP
Founder of Relationship Institute of the Rockies
Use QR code or visit **AlexAAvila.com**

BeMen is a call to action to offer fellowship, resources and support for the Gentleman, Hero & Warrior in all of us!

BeMen lives by a Code of Values
Known as The Warrior's Way.

BeMen life philosophy centers on
The Five Pillars of Male Wellness:

Emotional Intelligence
Financial Freedom
Mental Toughness
Physical Fitness
Spiritual Power

Join our growing community of like-minded,
extraordinary men who are focused on
making a positive impact in society!

www.facebook.com/groups/BeMenBrothers

www.BeMen.org

KIRK M SAMUELS

FOR YOUR
EYES
ONLY

The Inside Scoop About Men, *Porn,* and Marriage

Embodying
the Kings Code

LIVING THE
TRANSFORMATIVE LIFE

WRITTEN BY
PAULA BURT

IT'S NOT YOUR LIFE, IT'S YOU

A LAYMAN'S GUIDE TO THE POWER OF PERSPECTIVE

JASON KENDRICK

MEN, WOMEN & WALKING IN LOVE

How to
Win HER
&
Influence
HIM

THE ULTIMATE GUIDE TO UNDERSTANDING & FIXING RELATIONSHIP PROBLEMS

GENIE GOODWIN

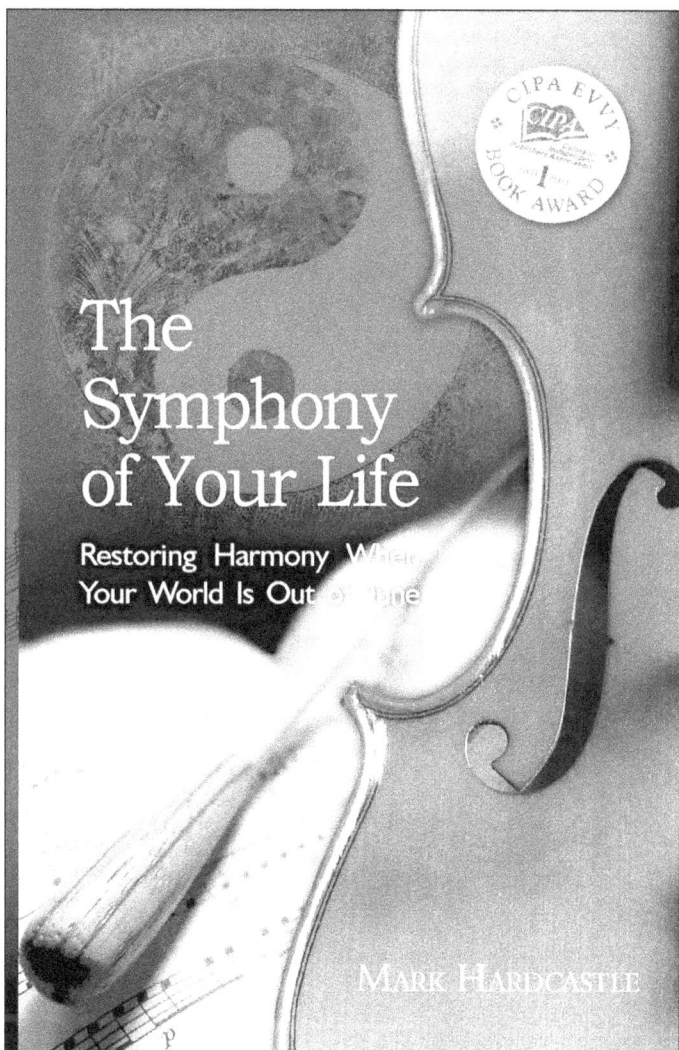

The
Symphony
of Your Life

Restoring Harmony When
Your World Is Out of Tune

MARK HARDCASTLE

BREAKING
THROUGH

3 Winning
Strategies to Create
Breakthrough
Results
in your Life,
Business and
Relationships

From a Master 8th
Degree Black Belt and
Transformational Coach

CHRIS NATZKE
CREATOR OF BLACK BELT LEADERSHIP

www.ingramcontent.com/pod-product-compliance
Lightning Source LLC
Chambersburg PA
CBHW022336280326
41934CB00006B/652